CALIFORNIA STATE UNIVERSITY, SACRAMENTO

This book is due on the last date stamped below.
Failure to return books on the date due will result in assessment
of overdue fees.

JEAN STAFFORD

GARLAND REFERENCE LIBRARY
OF THE HUMANITIES
(VOL. 377)

JEAN STAFFORD
A Comprehensive Bibliography

Wanda Avila

GARLAND PUBLISHING, INC. • NEW YORK & LONDON
1983

Acknowledgment is hereby made to the following periodicals
for permission to quote from articles by and about Jean
Stafford that were first published in their pages: *Commonweal,
Esquire, Kenyon Review, The New Republic, The New York Times, Vogue*
(Conde Nast Publications Inc.), and the Washington (D.C.) *Post.*

Library of Congress Cataloging in Publication Data

Avila, Wanda, 1939–
  Jean Stafford, a comprehensive bibliography.

  (Garland reference library of the humanities ;
v. 377)
  Includes index.
  1. Stafford, Jean, 1915——Bibliography.
I. Title. II. Series.
Z8833.3.A94 1983   [PS3569.T2]   016.813′54   82-49127
ISBN 0-8240-9210-4

Printed on acid-free, 250-year-life paper
Manufactured in the United States of America

CONTENTS

INTRODUCTION

Jean Stafford's work manifests two characteristic excellencies—a formidable irony and brilliant literary craftsmanship, the combination of these qualities leaving her with few equals among writers of the post-World-War-II generation. Yet, these are really not disparate qualities because the latter is the primary vehicle for the first. That is, in her fiction, Stafford's irony is not merely the result of plot, though situational ironies—especially those issuing from the incongruity between her protagonists' hopes, dreams, and expectations and their actual experience in modern America—do structure most of her plots. Nor is her irony merely the result of characterization, though her characters usually deviate radically from the American heroic ideal, and her protagonists are often painfully aware of the contrast between their aspirations to attain moral perfection and the reality of their inner corruption. Nor is her irony merely the result of theme, though her general theme, like that of so many of her contemporaries, is that the end of innocence has come to America.

More than in all of these ways, though, Stafford's irony is demonstrated in her attitude toward the failures and disappointments of her characters, and this attitude is revealed not so much in what she says but in how she says it. Stafford looks down with equanimity on the suffering of her protagonists, her auctorial voice suggesting that all this need not have been so had they relinquished their romantic illusions and been more tolerant of the limitations of themselves and of others and more accepting of the inevitable disappointments of life; that is, had they maintained their sense of irony. Stafford, herself, does maintain her sense of irony, expressed in her remarkably controlled style that makes her work so eminently readable.

I

In real life, Stafford found it rather more difficult to preserve her ironic aplomb. Born on July 1, 1915, in Covina, California, Stafford grew up in Boulder, Colorado, which she renamed "Adams" and used as a setting for much of her fiction. As a child, Stafford seems to have resembled the little girl protagonists who frequently appear in her stories—lonely, tomboyish, and pre-cocious. She showed a strong literary bent from an early age, her early poems and stories reflecting that incredible command of language which was later to distinguish her writing. In one of her early short stories, for example, she described her protago-nist as having "*oleaginous* black hair" (H4). By the time she was eleven, she had completed her first novel, a twelve-page thriller set in the British Museum, which she bound in cardboard and tied with rick-rack, and which she read over for a long time "at least once a day with undiminishing reverence" (A13).

Stafford's youthful ambition, however, was not to become a writer, but to become an acrobatic dancer and a Ph.D., although she eventually decided to limit herself to the latter goal. Accord-ingly, she earned B.A. and M.A. degrees at the University of Colorado, writing her Master's thesis on "Profane and Divine Love Motifs in English Literature of the 13th Century." After graduating in 1936, she studied philology at the University of Heidelberg for a year. Toward the end of her stay in Germany, she wrote back to a much admired professor, Miss McKeehan, at the University of Colorado, asking for a recommendation for a fellowship at some college for intellectual women, such as Radcliffe or Bryn Mawr. Stafford had to abandon her academic aspirations when Miss McKeehan answered that she did not believe that Stafford "had the makings of a scholar. 'Why don't you get married?' she said. 'Or, better, why don't you write?'" (C40)

Stafford did get married. In fact, she got married three times. In 1940, she married the poet Robert Lowell. Their stormy six-year marriage ended in an even stormier divorce in 1948. In 1950, she married Oliver Jensen, an editor for *Life* and co-head of Picture Press. This marriage lasted only a few months. (Dor-othea Straus has described Stafford and Jensen as being "like a couple cast in a performance of *Who's Afraid of Virginia Woolf?* for summer stock" [H11]). In 1959, she married A.J. Liebling, the *New Yorker* columnist and press critic; this marriage, too, was short-lived because Liebling died in 1963.

And Stafford did write. With the exception of a few sporadic attempts at teaching and lecturing, Stafford devoted her life to writing, producing three novels, fifty-one short stories, two nonfiction books, two juvenile books, and numerous articles, essays, reviews, and miscellaneous items. Her fiction earned her some popular and critical success and a number of awards, including the Pulitzer Prize for fiction in 1970. (Nevertheless, writers of lesser achievement have received more.)

Living most of her adult life in and around New York City, Stafford was very much a part of the New York literary world; yet she often felt herself somewhat of a "rube" among the New York Intellectuals. After Liebling's death, she retreated to their home on Fireplace Road in Springs, Long Island, where her delight in renovating and redecorating the house and in tending its gardens made her feel that, at last, she was "in the catbird seat" (C19).

As Stafford aged, she came more and more to resemble the bad-tempered old women who populate her fiction. Her increasing acerbity was undoubtedly the cumulative effect of a lifetime of frustrations and disappointments. Plagued by illnesses—physical and mental, real and imaginary—throughout her life, suffering from numerous failures in her emotional relationships from the time of early childhood, never receiving the recognition for her work she deserved, finding her creative powers blocked in her later years, Stafford experienced in 1977 the further indignity of a stroke that left her speechless. Stafford, whose facility with language had been so extraordinary, now found it difficult to utter even the simplest of thoughts. Nancy Flagg suggested to Stafford that her problem was psychosomatic because Stafford had written a story, "Beatrice Trueblood's Story," about a woman who wills herself deaf to avoid hearing what she does not want to hear. "Come clean, sister," said Flagg. "I'm on to your game. It's Beatrice Trueblood's story again. Okay, so you didn't believe it—you wrote it, and now you've done it. You can't speak because you find everything unspeakable. You can't talk because you see no one fit to talk to." In response, Stafford could only nod "her wonderful ravaged head" and laugh (H8).

When Stafford died on March 26, 1979, she left nothing to her family or many old friends, but willed everything—her money and personal possessions and the house and acreage in East Hampton—to her cleaning woman; Stafford even appointed this woman her literary executor. It is not clear whether Stafford intended this as a last gesture of defiance or as a very private joke.

II

Stafford's first novel, *Boston Adventure* (1944), brought forth astonished comparisons to the work of James, Austen, Dostoevsky, and, especially, Proust. Alfred Kazin, reviewing the book for the *New Republic*, was one of the many who pointed out its Proustian quality and called Stafford "an extraordinarily talented novelist" (G14). And Howard Mumford Jones, in the *Saturday Review*, recognized Stafford as "a commanding talent, who writes in the great tradition of the English novel"; he singled out for special praise the correspondence between the style and the sensibilities of the narrator of the story (G13).

Some reviews were, of course, mixed. Mina Curtiss, for example, in a review for the Boston *Globe*, acknowledged *Boston Adventure* as "an exceptionally clever first novel," but criticized its unauthentic picture of Boston, and argued that Stafford adopts some externals of Proust's method without adopting its essence (G8). Elizabeth Bullock, writing in the *Chicago Sun Book Week*, praised the book as a "fine psychological study, a triumph of stylistic virtuosity" but criticized the lack of resolution of the plot (G4). Diana Trilling, in *Nation*, called Stafford "a remarkable new talent" but found the second half of the book disappointing (G26).

The element of this novel which was almost unanimously praised was Stafford's elaborate and meticulous craftsmanship. It is this craftsmanship which still leads some readers to prefer *Boston Adventure* over her later novels; like Ihab Hassan, they continue to regard it as Stafford's "most impressive work" (F18).

In *The Mountain Lion* (1947), Stafford's second novel, the influence of Twain was most apparent, especially in its new element of humor. Consequently, most reviewers commented on how different it was from *Boston Adventure* but most concurred with Howard Mumford Jones, writing for the *New York Times Book Review*, that this second novel, though so different in setting, form, and style from Stafford's first, was "not a second-best novel" (G41). A few reviewers, like Ben Kartman in the *Chicago Sun Book Week*, did consider *The Mountain Lion* so inferior to *Boston Adventure* that Stafford, "for the sake of her literary prestige, should have kept [it] locked in her trunk" (G42). Others, like Henry Rago in *Commonweal*, considered it "an even finer novel" (G47).

As with *Boston Adventure*, the quality most often praised in *The Mountain Lion* was its style. Mark Schorer, for example, praised the novel in the *Kenyon Review* for its "demonstration of the first importance of style in fiction" (G49). Today, *The Mountain Lion* seems to be Stafford's most admired novel. Blanche H. Gelfant, in a *New Republic* review of the 1975 reissue of the book calls it a classic, in the sense that it is of high quality and in the sense that it is "basic, typical and enduring. . . . For it embodies our basic prejudices and enduring myths, and it represents our typical consciousness as Americans" (G37).

Stafford's third novel, *The Catherine Wheel*, also struck readers as being Jamesian, but the influence of Hawthorne, most notably, and of Eudora Welty and of Sarah Orne Jewett, to a lesser extent, gave this book a quite different character from Stafford's first two novels. A few reviewers, like Paul Engle in a review in the *Chicago Sunday Tribune Magazine of Books*, saw *The Catherine Wheel* as "further proof of the fictional and psychological brilliance of the author" (G55). However, most agreed with Irving Howe's judgment in the *Kenyon Review* that it was not "nearly so good as its predecessors"; Howe argued that here Stafford's "sensibility is so voracious that it consumes the story," and that her brilliant prose is "so fine and frequently so winning that it finally becomes a source of fascination in itself, undermining the matter it is supposed to reveal" (G60). And Charles J. Rolo, in the *Atlantic*, wrote that although this novel is "vastly superior to most current fiction," it is not so good as her first two novels:

"despite beautiful writing and meticulous craftsmanship, the novel seems a bit lacking in force and in size" (G71).

Suggestive of the contemporary attitude toward *The Catherine Wheel* is James Wolcott's recent review of the 1982 reissue of the novel by Ecco Press, as part of its "Neglected Books of the 20th Century" series. Wolcott argues that *The Catherine Wheel* "beats hollow nearly every novel published by a 'name' author in the post-World War II era." He wonders why, nevertheless, one hears so little about Stafford and suggests that "Perhaps Jean Stafford's reputation needs a central work to clinch a place for her in the ranks of the classic." He goes on to say that "if the republication of *The Catherine Wheel* doesn't assure her a top-flight berth, I don't know what will" (G81).

It was not until 1968 that Stafford began another novel, *The Parliament of Women* (first called *A Parlement of Fowles*). This, Stafford said, was to be the first autobiographical novel she had ever written (H7). Unfortunately, she was unable to complete it before her death. With the exception of two excerpts—"An Influx of Poets" (B48) and "Woden's Day" (B49)—none of this novel has been published.

Many readers consider Stafford an even better writer of short stories than of novels. Most of her stories have been collected in *Children Are Bored on Sunday* (1953), *Bad Characters* (1964), and *The Collected Stories* (1969), although fourteen remain uncollected. Indicative of the high quality of these stories is the fact that most of them were first published in such periodicals as *Harper's Bazaar*, *Harper's Magazine*, *Kenyon Review*, *Mademoiselle*, *Partisan Review*, *Sewanee Review*, and especially, the *New Yorker*. Also, a large number of them appeared in the *Best American Short Stories* and the *O. Henry Prize Stories* annual collections, as well as in numerous other anthologies. One of the stories, "In the Zoo," won first prize in the 1955 O. Henry Memorial Awards, and it was *The Collected Stories* that won Stafford the Pulitzer Prize in 1970.

Readers were almost unanimous in exclaiming over the craftsmanship of these stories, although some did object that the manner was too elaborate for the matter. With regard to *Children Are Bored on Sunday*, for example, Hansford Martin commented in the *Western Review* on the disjunction of form and content, saying that Stafford's words exert "an undue weight . . . upon a too frail substance of subject" (G91). Of *Bad Characters*, Jerome L.

Mazzaro, writing in the *Shenandoah,* criticized Stafford's over-emphasis on manner, saying that because of it the writing does not seem major (G147). And Morris Dickstein, reviewing *The Collected Stories* for the *New Republic,* praised them as "so gracefully professional, so eloquent and disciplined," but objected that "in the more serious stories, where deeper insight is demanded, style tends to expose itself as *mere* style" (G198).

However, wholly positive reviews far outnumbered the mixed reviews. Paul Engle, reviewing *Children Are Bored on Sunday* for the *Chicago Sunday Tribune Magazine of Books,* placed Stafford's stories "among the best that have been produced in this country," singling out for special praise her "firm imaginativeness of language" (G87). Granville Hicks, in the *Saturday Review,* was one of the many who praised the stories of *Bad Characters* as having "important themes, vivid characterization, and excellent craftsmanship" (G144). And Gene Baro, in the *New York Times Book Review,* exclaimed of these stories that "Jean Stafford is surely one of our best writers. She makes the English language a weapon or a wand" (G134). Of *The Collected Stories,* Pete Axthelm, in a *Newsweek* review, wrote that such is Stafford's technical virtuosity that this collection "could become a textbook for students of short fiction" (G190). Thomas Lask wrote in the New York *Times*: "If we consider anything before Donald Barthelme of value, we will herein find everything we desire in a collection of short stories" (G206). And Joyce Carol Oates, writing in the *Kenyon Review,* called *The Collected Stories* "a triumph of style and imagination. . . . These stories are achievements of art, short-story writing at its finest" (G212).

In the last fifteen years of her life, Stafford's failing creative powers and her precarious financial situation seem to have caused her to devote most of her energies to the writing of non-fiction, which she found more lucrative than fiction. With the exception of *An Etiquette for Writers* (which, in truth, is so short that it hardly counts as a book), the only non-fiction book Stafford wrote was *A Mother in History,* based on her interviews with Lee Harvey Oswald's mother. This book is probably Stafford's best-known work; it is certainly her most notorious. Reactions to *A Mother In History* were generally hostile. After the publication of a large part of it in *McCall's* (C10), Stafford said that she was "inundated by an avalanche of hate mail so impassioned and so various that I went quite funny in the head and took to wearing a false nose and a peculiar hat when I went to the supermarket or the hardware store" (C30).

Many reviewers, like Michael Christopher, writing for *U.S. Catholic*, found Stafford's injection of herself into the book "irritating and offensive. " Christopher argued that "Mrs. Oswald is perfectly able to damn herself; snide remarks and attempts to further prejudice the reader are inexcusable" (G161). John Gardner, in the *Southern Review*, called it a "tasteless book" and criticized Stafford for her superciliousness and emotional triviality and for selling out "to the snobbish, complacent, chattering ladies' magazines" (G165). Godfrey Hodgson, of the London *Observer*, commented that "This is a book about two women, and of the two I find Miss Stafford, with her knowing New York superiority and her lack of human sympathy, quite as chilling as the other" (G168).

On the other hand, some reviewers felt that Stafford had done an excellent job of reporting, and that the unpleasantness of the book was due solely to its subject matter—the personality of Mrs. Oswald. Reviewing the book for *Commonweal*, Jean Holzhauer commented, "Striving for objectivity, carefully crediting Mrs. Oswald with all her plausible abilities, Miss Stafford clearly remains a sensitive intelligence embarked on a distasteful assignment" (G169). An anonymous reviewer in *Newsweek* called the book "a masterpiece of character study and a gem of personal journalism" (G176). Marya Mannes, reviewing the book for *Book Week*, pointed out that Stafford "hardly speaks at all in the book," and saw it as "a triumph of control not only over material but over the writer's emotions" (G177). Karl Stern, in a *Critic* review, commented that "Miss Stafford writes with that elegant sparseness and controlled irony which we have come to admire in all her work" (G184). Finally, an anonymous reviewer for the *Virginia Quarterly Review* pointed out that, though most of the book is a transcript of Stafford's tape-recorded conversations with Mrs. Oswald, no one "but a skilled and sensitive novelist could have achieved this record, this insight" (G185).

The bulk of Stafford's non-fiction, however, consists of articles, essays, and reviews. Between 1969 and 1976, her articles and essays frequently appeared in such popular women's magazines as *Mademoiselle*, *McCall's*, and *Vogue*; she also wrote several essays for *Esquire*. The majority of her book reviews were published in *Vogue*, to which she contributed monthly and even bimonthly reviews from 1964 to 1974. Several of her reviews also appeared in *Esquire*, where she was book review editor from 1975 to 1976. In addition, she published many reviews in the *New York Review of Books*, *The New York Times Book Review*, and the Washington (D.C.) *Post Book World*.

Some of these works—such as "Why I Don't Get Around Much Anymore" (C35) and "The Eat Generation" (D3)—are hilariously funny. Most of the others will elicit at least a chuckle or two, certainly an occasional appreciative smile at the wit with which she treats her subject matter. A further interest offered by these pieces is the insight they provide into Stafford's life and personality and into the social and literary milieu in which she lived. Most of all, perhaps, they are interesting because of the way in which they are written.

In the style of her non-fiction, Stafford also reflects the influence of Henry James—in the elegance of her elaborate sentence structure and in her polysyllabic and recondite vocabulary; and the influence of Mark Twain—especially in her use of such colloquialisms as *grub, flummoxed, cornball, whim-whams, gosh darned, walloping, hornswoggled, highfalutin, shenanigans, conniption fits, high-tail it, give a hang, month of Sundays, cross as a bear, get my dander up, hell-bent-for-election*, and *going to hell in a handbasket*. How she combines these two styles can be seen in a quotation such as the following, from her review of John Barth's *Lost in the Funhouse*:

> Barth "presents fictions, ontological lucubrations, Homeric yarns in modern dress, and other works of nomenclature. One wishes one could join in the frolic because the author is having such a walloping good time with his distorting mirrors, ventriloquism, legerdemain, his pyrotechnics that combine girandoles of erudition with waggish pieces in the vernacular. But a good deal of the time one feels hornswoggled." (D47)

The amalgamation of two such distinct styles results in a style that is uniquely Stafford's. To describe this style, Howard Moss once quipped, "Think of Henry James being brought up in Colorado. . . ." (H9).

Unfortunately, Stafford's short non-fiction remains un-collected. Before she died, Stafford signed a contract for such a collection with Farrar, Straus and Giroux, and she compiled a tentative table of contents. Furthermore, it would seem that she intended the essay "Miss McKeehan's Pocketbook" (C40) as an introduction for such a book, but it has yet to appear.

III

In her fiction, Stafford takes an ironic view of the psychic terrain of America from the late 1920's through the 40's. She shows how the dream that all individuals can find a place in the world where they can live in harmony with society and with the dictates of the private self is unrealizable in the contemporary world. It was this dream which brought the Puritans to America and which took their descendants westward and which impels Stafford's twentieth-century Americans to traverse the ocean and the continent in search of a second chance.

Appropriately, then, the typical structure of Stafford's fiction parodies the quest-romance. That is, her characters leave home in search of fulfillment in a summer world, the world of ro-mance, which they usually believe they will find in Boston, the traditional center of American culture, or in the Far West, the reputed home of the true American spirit. However, they always find that the new world is as wintry as the home world, that it, too, is a world of satire and irony. No matter where they go, they encounter the same obstacles to their attainment of individual and social fulfillment. As a result, they find themselves forced either to abandon their claims to acceptance and recognition of their individuality or suffer loneliness, isolation, and alienation.

Appropriate, too, is the fact that Stafford's characters are pre-dominantly women and children, often girl children, childhood and virginity signifying the innocence with which these charac-ters begin their quest. Consequently, these characters function in Stafford's fiction as kind of Everyman, in the same way that the Jew and the Black function in so much other postwar fiction. Denied the love and acceptance which they seek, however, Stafford's characters do not maintain their innocence for long. Through their encounters with experience, they soon become as unloving, as cruel or as indifferent, as others have been to them. In Stafford's fiction, the sterility of the human heart in the modern world is effectively symbolized through her depiction of children as *enfants terribles* and of women as cruel, heartless mothers; or as childless wives, divorcees, or widows; or, and especially, as cold, unloving spinsters.

Boston Adventure, Stafford's first novel, demonstrates the process by which the idealistic, affectionate girl child can be transformed into a cynical, acerbic spinster. Sonia Marburg, the protagonist and first-person narrator of the novel, initially resembles Henry James's Isabel Archer, but the story she tells is no portrait of a lady. In this novel, Stafford, like James, dramatizes the encounter between innocence and experience in terms of the conflict between the American and the European. However, Stafford reverses the members of the equation by having the innocent European encounter experience in America. Sonia, the daughter of European immigrants, lives in Chichester, a suburb of Boston, whose name evokes the English town; she encounters experience in Boston, among the descendants of the Puritans.

Sonia's young life is made miserable by the poverty her German father imposes on the family through his laziness, and by the emotional turmoil her Russian mother constantly creates through her passionate tirades against her husband. The only happy times in Sonia's childhood occur when Miss Pride, an elderly, wealthy Boston spinster, comes each summer to vacation at the hotel where the nine-year-old Sonia works as a chambermaid. Because Miss Pride seems to embody the ordered and materially comfortable life Sonia desires, Sonia concocts a fantastic daydream in which Miss Pride adopts her and takes her across the bay that separates Chichester from Boston. Like her parents before her, like generations of other Europeans, like the Puritans themselves, then, Sonia looks to Boston for freedom from a life of poverty and oppression.

At the age of eighteen, her father having abandoned the family some years earlier, her brother dead, her mother in an insane asylum, Sonia stands alone in the world. However, she faces her future as confidently as Isabel Archer, determined to have the best for herself, "whether across the bay or across the ocean." And when Miss Pride does take her across the water to Boston, Sonia feels sure of the imminent fulfillment of her childhood dream. In Boston, however, she finds that Miss Pride has no intention of adopting her, the position of daughter being already filled by Hopestill Mather, Miss Pride's orphaned niece. On the contrary, Miss Pride regards Sonia more as a servant, and not as a particularly valued one at that. Furthermore, Sonia finds that in Boston the community of believers has been replaced by a community of socialites who visit one another's drawing rooms with the same fervor as that with which their ancestors went to church. Because having the proper surname alone predestines one to membership in this group, Sonia is as much a misfit in this world as she was in Chichester.

Sonia reacts to the frustration of her dream of finding a place in the world by willfully determining to achieve a place at any price. She does not make Isabel Archer's heroic renunciation but turns in envious hatred against Hopestill Mather, who occupies the place Sonia wants. Sonia's hatred is so intense that it leads to Hopestill's death, with the result that Sonia does then find her place in Miss Pride's house. But in killing Hopestill, Sonia kills the best part of herself, for the loving child she once was is replaced by a cynical, frigid twenty-one-year-old spinster, a youthful copy of the demonic Miss Pride. Thus, Sonia, aiming at self-definition but attaining only self-annihilation, is the first of those many Stafford protagonists whose innocence is corrupted by societal rejection.

The Mountain Lion, Stafford's second novel, deals with another blighted world from which the American dream of innocence has departed. This world is set, not in Boston, but in the Far West; and while the descendants of the Puritans figure in *Boston Adventure*, the descendants of the American pioneers figure in *The Mountain Lion*. Thus, it is Twain, not James, with whom Stafford dialogues in this novel.

The children Ralph and Molly Fawcett, the protagonists, seem, initially, to be Huckleberry Finn figures. Living with their widowed mother and their two older sisters in a middle-class home in Covina, California, their world resembles the genteel one that Twain so frequently satirized. The children's mother, hoping to make them conform to the stereotypes of "lady" and "gentleman," hedges their lives about with innumerable rules and restrictions. As a result, the children yearn to light out for the territory, which they believe is located at their uncle's ranch in Adams, Colorado—and the name "Adams" makes explicit the tradition in which Stafford is writing.

When Mrs. Fawcett finally allows the children to spend a summer at their uncle's ranch, they fully expect to find the glorious West of myth and legend. However, they are soon as disillusioned as Sonia Marburg was with Boston. Their biggest disappointment is that they are no more free to develop their potentialities in the Far West than they were at home. Ralph finds that the stereotypes have merely changed: in Covina, he was required to conform to the idea of gentleman; in the West, he must conform to the idea of cowboy. No one regards his reservations about total acceptance of either pattern with sympathy. Molly finds that to be accepted in the West, as in Covina, a girl must be as brainless as she is pretty. Since Molly is as intelligent as she is ugly, she is out of place in both worlds. Ralph resolves his dilemma by abandoning his desire for individuation and by trying to conform to his uncle's idea of a man; Molly rebels by directing a savage scorn toward everyone with whom she comes in contact. "By the end of the novel," as William T. Pilkington writes, "it is no longer possible to think of Molly as a female Huck Finn; she has been transformed into a young Miss Watson, complete with exacting morality" (F49). Both Ralph's conformity and Molly's rebellion result in the death of self, symbolized in the end by Ralph's shooting Molly in a hunting accident.

In *The Catherine Wheel*, Stafford's third and last novel, she further examines the consequences of rejection on the individual. Hawthorne, Maine, the setting of this novel, suggests at once its literary progenitor. And like *The Scarlet Letter*, it deals with the evil that can lurk behind the most innocent facade, and with the corrosive effects of hidden sin.

Like the previous two novels, *The Catherine Wheel* moves from summer to winter, from past to present, from dream to reality, from innocence to experience. The protagonist of the novel, Katharine Congreve, a beautiful, middle-aged spinster, spends each summer at her ancestral home in New England, the exquisite Congreve House, the gardens around which are said to be a "veritable paradise." Here Katharine has carefully preserved the innocent world of her youth, allowing few changes to be made in the house or in its customs, she herself continuing to dress and act as she had done as a girl. This Eden lacks only an Adam, but Katharine long ago cast John Shipley for this part, and has never given up that dream, even though he has been married for years to Katharine's cousin Maeve.

Having been rejected in love and never finding another man to replace John Shipley in her affections, Katharine has spent many years desiring revenge upon Maeve, the unwitting obstacle to Katharine's attainment of her dream. Katharine has always tried to suppress this envy and has so far succeeded that everyone regards her and the Shipleys as the best of friends, but her envy has grown over the years like an undetected cancer, "until its progress and its malevolent pain became the armature of her whole thought and conduct." But, by the end of the summer during which the novel takes place, Katharine has had to recognize that her dream is forever unattainable, that time has wrought many unpleasant changes in John Shipley, and that behind her own facade of beauty and innocence lies an abyss of ugliness and evil.

The events of the sub-plot of the novel parallel those of the main plot. The child Andrew Shipley, Katharine's cousin, also suffers rejection at the beginning of the summer during which the novel takes place; Victor Smithwick, the boy with whom he had always spent the summer in the past, has no time for Andrew this year because Victor's older brother Charles is home from the Navy. Andrew, having no other friends, then willfully hopes to regain Victor's friendship by wishing for the death of Charles. Although Andrew, like Katharine, feels guilty, knowing how unjust he is being, he cannot stifle the voice inside his head that obsessively chants, "Charles Smithwick, die."

Unable to relinquish their dreams and to reconcile themselves to reality, both Katharine and Andrew experience tragic consequences. Katharine can see death as the only solution to her dilemma, and fate obligingly arranges for her to be the victim of a freak accident. And Andrew, feeling that his hidden evil has caused Katharine's death, suffers psychic death, for it is implied that he—unlike Hawthorne's Pearl—is hereafter condemned to isolation, to live forever apart from human joy and sorrow, forever doing battle with the world, never to be a man in it.

Stafford's short stories, too, reflect Hawthorne's dark view of human nature, Twain's ironic view of America, and James's manner of narrating the complex fate of being an American. As in the novels, most of the characters in the short stories are in quest for a place in the world, a place where they can be accepted and valued for themselves. Stafford grouped the stories of *The Collected Stories* according to their geographical setting: Most of the stories under "Innocents Abroad" are set in Europe; the stories under "The Bostonians, and Other Manifestations of the American Scene" are set in Boston or Maine; the stories under "Cowboys and Indians, and Magic Mountains" are set in the Far West, and mainly in the semi-fictional small town of Adams, Colorado; and the stories included under "Manhattan Island" are set in New York City. In a sense, this geographical grouping, as Stafford admitted in her introductory note to *The Collected Stories*, is arbitrary because the final effect of her stories convinces that life is rather much the same everywhere: At home or abroad, in New England or the Far West, in the big city or small town, Stafford's Americans find that, in spite of some superficial differences in scenery, architecture, and manners, there is an underlying sameness to experience.

In another sense, though, this arrangement is not arbitrary. In the same introductory note, Stafford acknowledges Mark Twain and Henry James as two of her favorite authors, "to whose dislocation and whose sense of place" she feels allied (F10). And it is this sense of place and dislocation that her characters feel, no matter where they are, that makes the geographical arrangement, in an important sense, non-arbitrary. At home, in their place (typically the Far West), they find themselves in an impossible situation; they are oppressed, lonely, denied recognition as individuals. They yearn to go as far away as possible, like Polly Bay in "The Liberation," who leaves home shouting, "I hate, I despise, I abominate the West!" (B30). But when they arrive in the new city—Boston or New York or one in Europe, where they hope to find a new life, their sense of dislocation puts them in an equally impossible situation. Neither at home nor away from home can Stafford's characters find the freedom, sense of identity, or social fulfillment they seek. They remain lonely, alienated misfits, but they do not go home again.

Also, as in the novels, the protagonists of these stories are typically children and women who are unloved. Children suffer from the lack of parental love; young women despair of finding romantic love; wives are unloved by their husbands, and often end as divorcees or widows; aged spinsters look back on a loveless life. Furthermore, not only are these characters unloved, they are unloving. The horror of a world without love could be said to be the major theme of these stories, as it is of the novels.

Symbolic of the human being's sense of being helplessly alone in the world, unloved and unwanted, are the child protagonists of Stafford's stories. Often these children are orphans, like the two little girls in "In the Zoo" (B31). Other child protagonists have only one parent, usually an indifferent mother, like Ella in "The Darkening Moon" (B2). Even if the child has both parents, they are both likely to be insensible to their child's need for love, like Hannah's parents in "Cops and Robbers" (B29).

Some of Stafford's young women search in the larger world for a love to compensate for their lack of parental love. They are always disappointed. These young women yearn for parties and dates and are ignored, like Sue Ledbetter in "The Echo and the Nemesis" (B23); they fall in love and are scorned, like Pansy Venneman in "The Interior Castle" (B10). Sometimes one of them manages to become engaged, but before the wedding her fiancé dies, as happens in "The Liberation" (B30), or she discovers that he is a worthless creature whom she has deluded herself into believing she loved, as is the experience of the protagonist of "A Slight Manuever" (B13). Most frequently, Stafford's women remain spinsters. The middle-aged narrator of "I Love Someone," for example, says that she has lived the whole of her life in "the half-world of brief flirtations" and of friendships which "perished of the cold" or hung on "desiccated, outliving their meaning and never once realizing the possibility of love" (B27).

"Caveat Emptor" (B38) seems to be one of the very few exceptions to the generalization that dreams of romantic love are always defeated in Stafford's fiction. In this story, Victoria and Malcolm do find love; however, the story ends before they get married. If Victoria does marry, it is likely that she will soon find the misery most of Stafford's wives encounter. "A Country Love Story" (B20) and "An Influx of Poets" (B48), semifictional accounts of Stafford's own marriage to Robert Lowell, are typical in that they both show the devastating pain to which a woman exposes herself when she marries a man she loves.

The emotional sterility of these marriages is symbolized by the fact that they are usually childless and that the wives end as divorcees or young widows. In "A Modest Proposal," for example, several women wait out the six weeks before their divorces become final on a Caribbean island, finding the torpor of the island to be in perfect correlation with their psychological need "to repudiate struggle and to resume the earlier, easier indolence of lovelessness" (B19). And in "The Children's Game," Abby Reynolds, a young widow, has been living in Europe for nearly a year following the death of her husband, feeling that she has "become indistinguishable from the thousands and thousands of lonesome American ladies who lived abroad because a foreign address, however modest, had a cachet that a New York or a Boston apartment hotel did not." Many of these women are widows, like Abby, but all of them have spent "their lives leaning on someone—or being leaned on by—a father, a mother, a husband; and who, when the casket is closed or the divorce decree is final, find that they are waifs" (B43).

Typically, Stafford's unloved women become unloving. The length of the novel allowed Stafford to show this development in full, but in the short stories, she focuses on only one phase of this dehumanizing process. However, we can arrange these stories so that they, too, form a coherent narrative of the negative transformations of character brought about by rejection. Consider the following four stories as examples:

In "Cops and Robbers," Hannah, the five-year-old protagonist, loses her position as favored child in the family when her father takes her to his barber and has her beautiful blonde curls cut off in order to spite Hannah's mother. Her mother is then concerned not with Hannah's feelings but with the affront to herself; Hannah's father ignores her, gloating in his triumph; her brothers and sister treat her like a damaged piece of furniture. In resentment, Hannah begins to indulge in the fantasy of being an angry bee. If she were a bee, she thinks, she would sting not only her father and mother, brothers and sister, but also the barber and even the cat (B29). That is, the innocent as well as the guilty would all be victims of her aggression.

The protagonist of "Bad Characters" suggests what Hannah will be like in a few years. The narrator of this story has "an awful tongue." When she feels the urge to be alone, she lets fly, and none is ever more surprised than she when this "irrevocable slander, this terrible, talented invective" comes boiling out of her mouth (B33). What Hannah will be like as a mature woman is suggested by the character of the unhappy wife of "An Influx of Poets," who has "the tongue of an adder" and a heart "black with rage and hate" (B48). And perhaps she will end like old Miss Bellamy of "The Hope Chest" (B11), who lives in intolerable loneliness, yet who repels those few with whom she has contact by her heartless cruelty.

What kind of society is this in which children are discouraged and hindered from individuation? In which women, archetypal figures of fertility and rebirth, wander from place to place, never belonging, ever disvalued? A sick one, Stafford's fiction answers. The general malaise of contemporary American society is signified by the images of illness—both physical and mental—which characterize Stafford's fictional world. Especially frequent are numerous old people in various stages of invalidism and senility. In "Life Is No Abyss," a poor house is used as a microcosm of the world (the title is, needless to say, ironic); here young Lily Holmes, the protagonist, sees four long rows of beds, each one

> occupied by an ancient, twisted woman; the humps of their withered bodies under the seersucker coverlets looked truncated and deformed like amputated limbs or mounds of broken bones, and the wintry faces that stared from the stingy pillows had lost particularity: among them it would have been impossible to determine which was primarily bleak or mean or brave or imbecile, for age and humiliation had blurred the predominant humor and had all but erased the countenance. (B26)

The most common disease suffered is tuberculosis. Although Stafford's tuberculars are found everywhere, they figure primarily in the stories set in Colorado, which is especially ironic because the West—traditionally seen as the source of health for the republic—is populated by dying tuberculars. So pervasive is the illness of the society in which Stafford's protagonists live that they, naturally, come to see their own health as a liability, a sign of their unacceptability and inadequacy. For example, the little protagonist of "The Healthiest Girl in Town" feels "bovine in the midst of nymphs [her tubercular girlfriends]" and yearns to be able to say to them, "I can't come to your house this afternoon. I have to have an X-ray" (B24).

There are various other instances of disease and pain in these stories: In "A Summer Day," Jim Littlefield finds that there is an epidemic, caused by poisoned water, sweeping the orphanage where he is now to make his home (B16). The elderly gentleman who wishes to attract Rose Fabrizio, the protagonist of "The Bleeding Heart," offers, as a seductive ploy, to show her on his breast "the most unsightly wen you ever saw" (B15). In order to preserve her reputation as a beauty, by which she has attained at least a modicum of acceptance by society, Angelica Early in "The End of a Career" goes each year to a sanitarium to have her face "planed away with a steel-wire brush, electrically propelled," for days and even weeks thereafter suffering drastic, sickening pain as she waits for "the scabs that encrusted her flensed skin" to disappear (B37). The story "The Interior Castle" is the account of Pansy Vanneman's nose operation, performed without benefit of anesthesia (B10).

Not surprisingly, the attempts of the protagonists of these stories to adjust to the world in which they live often result in their mental illness. Beatrice Trueblood, for example, in "Beatrice Trueblood's Story" (B34) reacts with psychosomatic deafness to the bad temper of her husbands. Cora Savage, in "An Influx of Poets" (B48), develops psychosomatic headaches in response to her marital problems. Mrs. Mark Kimball, in "The Warlock" (B36), suffers a nervous breakdown after her husband divorces her. When Emily of "Children Are Bored on Sunday" meets up with Alfred Eisenburg, she is recovering from a nervous breakdown brought on by "months of spreading, cancerous distrust, of anger that made her seasick, of grief that shook her like an influenza chill, of the physical afflictions by which the poor victimized spirit sought vainly to wreck the arrogantly healthy flesh." Alfred, too, has recently gone through a similar experience, so that the two immediately recognize in each other a "cousin-german in the territory of despair" (B14). As William Peden has said, Stafford's world is "one into which sunlight and fresh air seldom penetrate; the odor of death hovers over it" (G94).

The cataclysmic events leading up to and surrounding World War II also function as emblems of modern society's hostility to the individual. While Stafford never deals with the War directly, it functions as the background of many of her stories, such as "The Home Front" (B7), "The Captain's Gift" (B9), "A Winter's Tale" (B32), "The Maiden" (B21), and "My Blithe, Sad Bird" (B41). These stories all show that the real war takes place not on the front lines but at home, not in the heads of military strategists but in the hearts of ordinary individuals, and its toll is manifested not only in dead bodies and destroyed cities but in dead spirits and destroyed lives.

Stafford's fiction offers no hope that society can ever be changed, and her characters are seldom able to effect a satisfactory solution to their feelings of dislocation, alienation, and loneliness. However, Stafford herself regards their plight with the equanimity of the ironic observer—detached, objective, intellectual, and reflective. This, she suggests through her manner of narration, is the only way in which the individual can be reconciled to the inevitable disappointments of life.

Stafford's emotional detachment has frequently been commented upon; but while her freedom from sentimentality and self-pity have been praised, her "studious detachment" (G154) has, more frequently perhaps, been criticized. For example, *Boston Adventure* was disparaged for its lack of passionate intensity (G27). In *The Mountain Lion*, Stafford's emotional detachment suggested that she felt "unpleasantly superior to her characters as though she were inviting the reader to join her in mildly ridiculing them" (G36). *The Catherine Wheel* was said to lack "emotional immediacy" (G78). The stories of *Children Are Bored on Sunday* were found to have a "cold brilliance and implacable finality" (G90); to be "without sentimental garnish, perhaps equally without the warmth of human sympathy" (G96). In *A Winter's Tale*, Stafford's detachment is described as "clinical," because it "makes little attempt to involve the reader's sympathetic concern for the characters" (G110). The stories in *Bad Characters* were said to demonstrate again Stafford's "well-known caustic wit, bitterness and jaundiced view of humanity" (G133). "Chilling" was the adjective used again and again to describe *A Mother in History*, and some readers found Stafford in this book to carry "detachment to the brink of contempt and sometimes beyond it" (G168). And *The Collected Stories* were said to want passion, involvement, and intensity (G216), and to have an "icy privacy" (G200). However, Stafford's unremitting irony precludes the kind of emotional involvement which these comments reveal most readers to expect in fiction. By another author, Stafford's characters would arouse the reader's pity, but Stafford "keeps her respectful distance, and so may we" (G202).

Stafford's detachment is integrally connected with her objectivity. Apart from her concern with craftsmanship, Stafford's objectivity is manifested both in her refusal to judge her characters and in her keen attention to material reality. In her paper on "The Psychological Novel," Stafford argues vehemently for the importance of objectivity in the writer. She praises Dostoyevsky, Austen, and Flaubert, especially, because they "remain impartial and do not sit in moral judgment upon their created people but allow the reader to draw his own conclusions" (C1). How successful Stafford was at attaining this objectivity in her own work is indicated by the frequent praise of her "vivid presentation of truth without moral judgment" (H74).

The other aspect of her objectivity is her fascination "with the material objects of daily, sensory existence" (F37), objects which she often imbues with symbolic significance. Some readers have even felt that her use of "sensitively observed detail" (G39) is excessive; as one reviewer wrote, her "truly feminine absorption in detail" makes her seem sometimes "to be writing for visitors from Mars" (G125). This attention to detail, though, is the primary means by which Stafford signals her respect for reality, grim though it may be, and her antagonism to the illusions by which the romantic attempts to escape from that reality.

A third aspect of Stafford's ironic voice is her intellectuality. When one reads Stafford, one has no doubt that she is a person of superior intelligence who has read widely and well and who has thought deeply about experience. This intellectuality manifests itself in her wit, in her many allusions to a wide variety of literary and philosophical works, in her elaborate syntax with its frequent employment of rhetorical figures, and above all in her vocabulary: words such as *ichneumon, teratological, ailurophile, eleemosynary, sesquipedalia, aestivating,* and *anthropophagous* stud her sentences.

Closely related to her intellectuality is her reflectiveness. Stafford's main interest is never in what her characters do or in how they feel but in why they do what they do or why they feel as they do. Consequently, it has frequently been said that her "strength is psychological analysis" (G50) and that she has "an intensely introspective, feminine sensibility" (G190). A comment which Joyce Carol Oates made with regard to Stafford's stories, and which links up Stafford's reflectiveness with her objectivity, applies to most of Stafford's works: "This is an art that curves inward toward the meditative, the reminiscent, given life not by bold gestures or strokes but by a patient accumulation of sharply-observed impressions: the wealth of a poet's eye, or a painter's" (F28).

In sum, Stafford's characters are seldom able to resolve the conflict between their dreams of love, of belonging, and the reality of their rejection by their society; consequently, their struggle to actualize their dreams results only in disillusionment and suffering. There is a way out, though, Stafford's auctorial voice suggests, and that is to transcend the immediate and experiential by adopting the stance of the ironic observer—reflective, objective, intellectual, and, above all, emotionally detached.

III

In spite of the significance of Stafford's work, she has received comparatively little critical attention. Although such critics as Ihab Hassan (F17) and Olga Vickery (F40, F41) insisted, years ago, that Stafford merits considerable attention, she remains, as one recent reviewer put it, "one of the truly great underrateds" (G81). It is especially surprising that there has been no previous extensive listing of writings by and about Jean Stafford. The few bibliographical listings that do exist are extremely scanty, seldom going beyond a list of her books and a few secondary sources. This bibliography is an attempt to remedy this neglect, and it is hoped that it will foster a greater appreciation of the many facets of Stafford's literary achievement.

This bibliography is divided into two parts: Part I lists all published, indexed works by Jean Stafford; Part II lists all works about her. Part I is further divided into (A) books—subdivided into novels, novellas, collections, juvenile books, and nonfiction books; (B) short stories; (C) articles and essays; (D) book and movie reviews; and (E) miscellanea. All items of Part I are listed in chronological order by initial publication; all later reprintings are also listed. Part II is further divided into (F) criticism on Stafford—subdivided into general criticism, criticism of individual works, foreign criticism, and dissertations; (G) reviews of eleven of Stafford's books; and (H) bio-bibliographical material subdivided into articles, interviews, and reminiscences; references to Stafford in books primarily about others; newspaper stories, editorials, and letters to the editor; articles in reference books; biographical notes in collections; and obituaries. Most of the items of Part II are listed in alphabetical order by the author's last name, though most of the items in Section H are listed in chronological order. A comprehensive author, title, and subject index is included at the end of the bibliography.

Not listed herein are several published works by and about Stafford which have not been indexed. The works by her include two short stories: "Mountain Jim" (*Boy's Life* [Feb. 1968]) and an excerpt from *The Catherine Wheel* (*Harper's Bazaar* [Dec. 1951]); ten essays: four introductions to books and catalogues and six essays published in *Mademoiselle* (May 1950, Dec. 1951, and July 1952), *Vogue* (15 Oct. 1947), *Junior Bazaar* (Dec. 1947), and *Newsday* (13 May 1973); and fifty-one reviews, all but thirteen of which appeared in the Washington (D.C.) *Post Book World* between 1967 and 1974. The unindexed works about Stafford include several articles and hundreds of reviews of her books, published in small newspapers around the country. Of the articles, the most interesting are the interviews published in the

New York *World-Telegram* (5 Dec. 1947), *The American Weekly* (22 Aug. 1948), *The Bridgeport Post* (13 Jan. 1952), *Women's Wear Daily* (22 May 1969), and the *Barnard Bulletin* (10 March 1971). Tear sheets and clippings of these works are in the Jean Stafford Collection at the University of Colorado in Boulder, where I became aware of their existence. Unfortunately, this Collection was not available for examination before I had finished this bibliography.

Also not listed herein are any of Stafford's unpublished works, including her lectures, letters, and manuscripts, most of which can be found in the University of Colorado Collection. Otherwise, an attempt has been made to give a complete and accurate list of everything that has been published by or about Jean Stafford. I regret any of the perhaps inevitable omissions and inaccuracies that occur herein.

Among the many librarians and libraries who have assisted me in compiling this bibliography, I owe my greatest debt to Sonia Jacobs, Dinah McKay, and Nora Quinlan, of the Rare Books Room at the University of Colorado at Boulder; and to the staffs of the Library of Congress, the University of Maryland Library, and the George Mason University Library (and particularly to Linda A. Miller of Interlibrary Loans). I would also like to express my appreciation to the many people who answered my queries, including Robert Giroux, Joan Massey, and Chael Graham of Farrar, Straus and Giroux; Shirley Connell of *Vogue*; Lietta Dwork of *Ladies' Home Journal*; Rodney G. Dennis, Curator of Manuscripts, the Houghton Library, Harvard University; Sonia L. Jacobs, Acting Head, Special Collections Department, University of Colorado Library at Boulder; and, especially, C. David Heymann (*American Aristocracy* [New York: Dodd, Mead, 1980]). In addition, I would like to thank Jackson Bryer and Kathleen Field for their secondary bibliography on Carson McCullers (New York: Garland, 1980), which helped me decide many questions about the format of this bibliography. I would also like to thank Sandy Slater of George Mason University's Word Processing Center for her assistance in the preparation of this manuscript. Finally, I am most grateful to Julia Johnson, my editor, and to Kathryn Hilt of Bernard Baruch College for her advice and encouragement.

CHRONOLOGY OF
IMPORTANT DATES

1915   Born July 1 in Covina, California. Fourth child of
            John Richard and Mary Ethel (McKillop) Stafford.

1925   Stafford family moves to Boulder, Colorado.

1936   Takes B.A. and M.A. from the University of Colo-
            rado.

1936-37   Studies philology at the University of Heidelberg.

1937-38   Instructor at Stephens College in Columbus, Mis-
            souri.

1939   Publishes first short story, "And Lots of Solid
            Color," in *American Prefaces*.

1940   Marries Robert Lowell, April 2.

1940-41   Works as secretary for the *Southern Review*, Baton
            Rouge, Louisiana.

1941-42   Works part-time as secretary at Sheed and Ward,
            New York City.

1942-43   Stafford and Lowell live with Tates in Monteagle,
            Tennessee.

1943   Spends summer at Yaddo. Joins Lowell in New York
            in September. Lowell is imprisoned for draft evasion
            in October.

1944   In spring, moves to Black Rock, Connecticut, to be
            with Lowell while he serves out his parole. In
            November, Stafford and Lowell move to Westport,
            Connecticut. Publishes first novel, *Boston Adventure*.
            Receives *Mademoiselle's* Merit Award. Becomes
            Member of Cosmopolitan Club (New York).

1945   Awarded National Institute of Arts and Letters grant
            in literature. Awarded a Guggenheim fellowship in
            fiction. Lecturer at Queens College (now Queens

	College of the City University of New York). Buys house in Damariscotta Mills, Maine.
1946	Separates from Lowell in September.
1947	Publishes *The Mountain Lion*.
1948	Divorces Lowell in April. Awarded Guggenheim fellowship in fiction. Receives National Press Club Award.
1950	Marries Oliver Jensen, January 28.
1952	Publishes The *Catherine Wheel*. Publishes *An Etiquette for Writers: 1952 Writers' Conference in the Rocky Mountains*.
1953	Publishes *Children Are Bored on Sunday*. Publishes *The Interior Castle*. Divorces Oliver Jensen.
1954	Publishes *A Winter's Tale* in *New Short Novels* (with others).
1955	Receives O. Henry Memorial Award for best short story of the year, "In the Zoo."
1956	Publishes *Stories* (with others).
1959	Marries A.J. Liebling, April 3.
1962	Publishes *Arabian Nights*. Publishes *Elephi, the Cat with the High I.Q.*
1963	Liebling dies, December 21.
1964-65	Fellow, Center for Advanced Studies, Wesleyan University.
1964	Publishes *Bad Characters*.
1965	Receives grant from Rockefeller Foundation.
1966	Publishes *A Mother in History*. Publishes *Selected Stories of Jean Stafford*.
1967-69	Adjunct professor at Columbia University.
1969	Publishes *The Collected Stories*. Receives Ingram-Merrill grant. Receives Chapelbrook grant.
1970	Receives Pulitzer Prize for fiction. Member, National Institute of Arts and Letters (New York City).
1979	Dies in White Plains, New York, March 26. Her ashes placed in Greenriver Cemetery in East Hampton, Long Island, beside the body of A.J. Liebling, April 10.

ABBREVIATIONS

BA	*Boston Adventure*
BC	*Bad Characters*
CABS	*Children Are Bored on Sunday*
CS	*The Collected Stories*
CW	*The Catherine Wheel*
MH	*A Mother in History*
ML	*The Mountain Lion*
S	*Stories*
SS	*Selected Stories by Jean Stafford*
WT	*A Winter's Tale*

Part I
Works by Jean Stafford

SECTION A

BOOKS

This section lists all editions of Jean Stafford's (1) novels, (2) novellas, (3) collections, (4) juvenile books, and (5) non-fiction books. The books in each subsection are listed in chronological order. First editions, paperbacks, and translations have been so identified. Most editions have been personally verified, but some could be verified only through *Cumulative Books in Print, The National Union Catalogue, Index Translationum,* or an OCLC computer terminal.

I. NOVELS

A1 *Boston Adventure* (1944)

New York: Harcourt, Brace, 1944 (first edition).
New York: Harcourt, Brace, 1944 (paperback).
Philadelphia: Blakiston, 1944.
Toronto: McLeod, 1944.
London: Faber and Faber, 1946.
Garden City, New York: Sun Dial, 1946 (paperback).
Toronto: Blue Ribbon, 1946 (paperback).
Paris: Editions de la Paix, 1949, 2 vol. (tr. as *Le Cage D'Or* by Jean Poumarat).
In *The Interior Castle*. New York: Harcourt, Brace, 1953. (See A6.)
New York: Dell, 1960 (paperback).
New York: Harcourt, Brace, 1967 (paperback).

A2 *The Mountain Lion* (1947)

New York: Harcourt, Brace, 1947 (first edition).
New York: Random, 1947.
Toronto: McLeod, 1947.
London: Faber and Faber, 1948.
Stockholm: A. Bonnier, 1949 (tr. as *Puman*; inscribed "Cecile Starr").
Copenhagen: Glydenal, 1950 (tr. as *Bjergløven* by Merete Engberg).
In *The Interior Castle*. New York: Harcourt, Brace, 1953. (See A6.)
Cologne and Zurich: Benziger Verlag, 1958 (tr. as *Die Geschwister* by Elisabeth Schnack).
New York: Popular Library, 1962 (paperback).
Toronto: Random, 1962.
New York: Random, 1962.
New York: Farrar, Straus and Giroux, 1972.
Albuquerque: University of New Mexico Press, 1977; intro. by William T. Pilkington (paperback).
New York: Dutton, 1983 (paperback).

A3   *The Catherine Wheel* (1952)

New York: Harcourt, Brace, 1952 (first edition).
New York: Random, 1952.
Toronto: McLeod, 1952.
London: Eyre and Spottiswode, 1952.
Cologne and Zurich: Benziger Verlag, 1959 (tr. as
    Das Katharinenrad by Elisabeth Schnack).
New York: Avon, 1966 (paperback).
New York: Manor, 1974 (paperback).
New York: Ecco, 1981 (Neglected Books of the 20th
    Century Series; paperback).

2. NOVELLAS

A4   *A Winter's Tale* (1954)

In *New Short Novels* (by Jean Stafford, Elizabeth
    Etnier, Shelby Foote, and Clyde Miller). Vol. I.
    Ed. Mary Louise Aswell. New York: Ballantine,
    1954 (first edition).
Toronto: T. Allen, 1954.
London: Gollancz, 1959.
Cologne and Zurich: Benzinger Verlag, 1960 (tr. as
    Ein Wintermärchen, und andere Erzählungen by
    Elisabeth Schnack).
In *Bad Characters*. New York: Farrar, Straus and
    Giroux, 1964. (See A8.)
In Selected Stories of Jean Stafford. New York: New
    American, 1966 (paperback). (See A9.)

3. COLLECTIONS

A5   *Children Are Bored on Sunday* (1953)

New York: Harcourt, Brace, 1953 (first edition).
New York: Random, 1953.
In *The Interior Castle*. New York: Harcourt, Brace,
    1953. (See A6.)
London: Gollancz, 1954.

Contains "The Echo and the Nemesis," "A Country Love Story," "A Summer Day," "The Maiden," "The Home Front," "Between the Porch and the Altar," "The Bleeding Heart," "The Interior Castle," "A Modest Proposal," and "Children Are Bored on Sunday."

A6 *The Interior Castle* (1953)

New York: Harcourt, Brace, 1953.

Contains *Boston Adventure, The Mountain Lion,* and *Children Are Bored on Sunday.*

A7 *Stories* (with John Cheever, Daniel Fuchs, and William Maxwell, 1953)

New York: Farrar, Straus, and Cudahy, 1956.
London: Gollancz, 1957 (entitled *A Book of Stories*).
Ontario: Ambassador, 1957.
New York: Farrar, Straus and Giroux, 1966; intro. by William Peden.
New York: Noonday, 1966; intro. by William Peden (paperback).

Contains "The Liberation," "In the Zoo," "Bad Characters," "Beatrice Trueblood's Story," and "Maggie Meriwether's Rich Experience."

A8 *Bad Characters* (1964)

New York: Farrar, 1964 (first edition).
Ontario: Ambassador, 1964.
London: Chatto and Windus, 1965.

Contains "Bad Characters," "The End of a Career," "A Reasonable Facsimile," "In the Zoo," "Cops and Robbers," "The Liberation," "The Captain's Gift," "A Reading Problem," "Caveat Emptor," and "A Winter's Tale."

A9 *Selected Stories of Jean Stafford* (1966)

New York: New American, 1966 (paperback).

Contains "The Echo and the Nemesis," "A Country Love
Story," "A Summer Day," "The Maiden," "The Home Front,"
"A Modest Proposal," "Children Are Bored on Sunday,"
"Bad Characters," "The End of a Career," "A Reasonable
Facsimile," "Cops and Robbers," "The Liberation," "The
Captain's Gift," "Caveat Emptor," "A Winter's Tale,"
and "Beatrice Trueblood's Story."

A10   *The Collected Stories* (1969)

New York: Farrar, Straus and Giroux, 1969 (first
    edition).
New York: Farrar, Straus and Giroux, 1969
    (paperback).
London: Chatto and Windus, 1970.
Paris: Stock, 1971 (tr. as *Le Coffre Aux Espérances*
    by Jean-Gerard Chauffeteau).
Franklin Center, Pa.: Franklin Library, 1979
    (limited edition); illustrated by Barron Storey.
New York: Farrar, Straus and Giroux, 1980.
New York: Farrar, Straus and Giroux, 1980
    (paperback).

Contains THE INNOCENTS ABROAD: "Maggie Meriwether's
Rich Experience," "The Children's Game," "The Echo and
the Nemesis," "The Maiden," "A Modest Proposal," and
"Caveat Emptor"; THE BOSTONIANS, AND OTHER
MANIFESTATIONS OF THE AMERICAN SCENE: "Life Is No
Abyss," "The Hope Chest," "Polite Conversation," "A
Country Love Story," "The Bleeding Heart," "The Lippia
Lawn," and "The Interior Castle"; COWBOYS AND INDIANS,
AND MAGIC MOUNTAINS: "The Healthiest Girl in Town,"
"The Tea Time of Stouthearted Ladies," "The Mountain
Day," "The Darkening Moon," "Bad Characters," "In the
Zoo," "The Liberation," "A Reading Problem," "A Summer
Day," and "The Philosophy Lesson"; MANHATTAN ISLAND:
"Children Are Bored on Sunday," "Beatrice Trueblood's
Story," "Between the Porch and the Altar," "I Love
Someone," "Cops and Robbers," "The Captain's Gift," and
"The End of a Career."

4. JUVENILE

A11   *Elephi: The Cat with the High I.Q.* (1962)

New York: Farrar, Straus and Cudahy, 1962 (first
      edition).
Ontario: Ambassador, 1962.
New York: Dell, 1966 (paperback).

A12   *Arabian Nights: The Lion and the Carpenter and Other*
Tales from the Arabian Nights, Retold (1962)

New York: Macmillan, 1962.
London: Macmillan, 1962.
New York: Macmillan, 1963.

Contains "Prince Kamar Al-Zaman and Princess Budur,"
"The Sandalwood Merchant and the Sharpers," "The Lion
and the Carpenter," and "The Story of Abu-Kir and Abu-
Sir."

5. NON-FICTION

A13   *An Etiquette for Writers: 1952 Writers' Conference in*
the Rocky Mountains (1952)

Boulder: University of Colorado, 1952.

Transcript of a speech Stafford delivered at the 1952
Writers' Conference at the University of Colorado at
Boulder in 1952. It is 12 pages (approximately 6,000
words) long.

A14   *A Mother in History* (1966)

New York: Farrar, Straus and Giroux, 1966.
London: Chatto and Windus, 1966.
Ontario: Ambassador, 1966.
New York: Bantam, 1966 (paperback).

Paris: Éditions de Trevise, 1968 (tr. as *La Mère
   D'Oswald Parle* by Jeanne Fournier-Pargoire).

A large part of this book was first published as "The
Strange World of Marguerite Oswald" (*McCall's*, 93 [Oct.
1965]); see C10.

SECTION B

SHORT STORIES

This section lists Stafford's short stories in chronological order by their initial publication. Later reprintings are also given, first in works by Stafford, and then in works by others.

1939

B1 "And Lots of Solid Color." *American Prefaces*, 5 (Nov.
1939), pp. 22-25.

1944

B2 "The Darkening Moon." *Harper's Bazaar*, 78 (Jan. 1944),
60, 96-98, 100.

In *CS*, pp. 251-62.

B3 "The Lippia Lawn." *Kenyon Review*, 6 (Spring 1944),
237-45. Signed "Phoebe Lowell."

In *CS*, pp. 171-78.

B4 "The Wedding: Beacon Hill." (Excerpt from the novel
Boston Adventure.) *Harper's Bazaar*, 78 (June 1944),
pp. 48-50, 84-94.

Rpt. *The Best American Short Stories, 1945*. Ed. Martha
Foley. Boston: Houghton Mifflin, 1945, pp. 257-71.

Rpt. *200 Years of Great American Short Stories*. Ed.
Martha Foley. Boston: Houghton Mifflin, 1975, pp. 732-
43.

B5 "Hotel Barstow." (Excerpt from the novel *Boston
Adventure*.) *Partisan Review*, 11 (Summer 1944), 243-64.

B6 "A Reunion." *Partisan Review*, 11 (Fall 1944), 423-27.

Rpt. *Anchor in the Sea: An Anthology of Psychological
Fiction*. Ed. Alan Swallow. New York: William Morrow,
1947, pp. 102-10.

Rpt. *A Book of Stories*. Ed. Royal Alfred Gettman and
Bruce Harkness. New York: Holt, Rinehart and Winston,
1955, pp. 351-56.

1945

B7 "The Home Front." *Partisan Review,* 12 (Spring 1945),
    149-69.

    In *CABS,* pp. 104-42; *SS,* pp. 60-81.

    Rpt. *Autumn Light: Illuminations of Age.* Ed. L.M.
    Schulman. New York: Crowell, 1978, pp. 49-88.

B8 "Between the Porch and the Altar." *Harper's,* 190 (June
    1945), 654-57.

    In *CABS,* pp. 144-55; *CS,* pp. 407-13.

1946

B9 "The Captain's Gift."   (Originally published as "The
    Present.") *Sewanee Review,* 54 (April 1946), 206-15.

    In *BC,* pp. 16-72; *SS,* pp. 181-88; *CS,* pp. 437-45.

B10 "The Interior Castle." *Partisan Review,* 13 (Nov.-Dec.
    1946), 519-32.

    In *CABS,* pp. 194-217; *CS,* pp. 179-93.

    Rpt. *The Best American Short Stories, 1947.* Ed. Martha
    Foley. Boston: Houghton Mifflin, 1947, pp. 416-32.

    Rpt. *The Best of the Best American Short Stories, 1915-
    1950.*   Ed. Martha Foley.   Boston: Houghton Mifflin,
    1950, pp. 263-78.

    Rpt. *Stories of Modern America.* Ed. Herbert Gold and
    David L. Stevenson. New York: St. Martin's, 1961, pp.
    337-51.

    Rpt. *The World of Modern Fiction.* Ed. Steven Marcus.
    New York: Simon & Schuster, 1966, pp. 199-212.

    Rpt. *American Short Stories Since 1945.* Ed. John
    Hollander. New York: Harper & Row, 1968, pp. 56-72.

1947

B11 "The Hope Chest." *Harper's*, 194 (Jan. 1947), 62-65.

In *CS*, pp. 113-32.

Rpt. *Prize Stories of 1947: The O. Henry Awards.* Ed. Herschel Brickell. Garden City, New York: Doubleday, 1947, pp. 240-45.

B12 "The Tunnel with No End." (Excerpt from the novel *The Mountain Lion.*) *Harper's Bazaar*, 81 (Jan. 1947), 102, 153-56.

B13 "A Slight Manuever." *Mademoiselle*, 24 (Feb. 1947), 177, 282-87, 289.

1948

B14 "Children Are Bored on Sunday." *New Yorker*, 23 (21 Feb. 1948), 23-26.

In *CABS*, pp. 236-52; *SS*, 91-100; *CS*, pp. 373-83.

Rpt. *The Best American Short Stories of 1949.* Ed. Martha Foley. Boston: Houghton Mifflin, 1949, pp. 295-304.

Rpt. *The Short Story.* Ed. James B. Hall and Joseph Langland. New York: Macmillan, 1956, pp. 348-57.

Rpt. *55 Short Stories from the* New Yorker. New York: Simon & Schuster, 1949, pp. 245-54.

Rpt. *Fifty Best American Short Stories, 1915-1965.* Ed. Martha Foley. Boston: Houghton Mifflin, 1965, pp. 397-406.

B15 "The Bleeding Heart." *Partisan Review*, 15 (Sept. 1948), 974-96.

In *CABS*, pp. 156-92; *CS*, pp. 147-69.

B16 "A Summer Day." *New Yorker*, 24 (11 Sept. 1948), 29-35.

In *CABS*, pp. 62-85; *SS*, 39-50; *CS*, pp. 345-59.

Rpt. *Prize Stories of 1949: The O. Henry Awards.* Ed. Herschel Brickell. Garden City, New York: Doubleday, 1949, pp. 262-75.

Rpt. *Masters of the Modern Short Story.* Ed. Walter Havighurst. New York: Harcourt, 1955, pp. 438-53.

1949

B17 "The Cavalier." *New Yorker*, 24 (12 Feb. 1949), 28-36.

B18 "Polite Conversation." *New Yorker*, 25 (20 Aug. 1949), 24-28.

In *CS*, pp. 121-32.

B19 "A Modest Proposal." (Originally published as "Pax Vobiscum.") *New Yorker*, 25 (23 July 1949), 21-24.

In *CABS*, pp. 218-34; *SS*, pp. 82-90; *CS*, pp. 65-74.

1950

B20 "A Country Love Story." *New Yorker*, 26 (6 May 1950), 26-31.

In *CABS*, pp. 40-60; *SS*, pp. 26-37; *CS*, pp. 133-45.

Rpt. *Prize Stories of 1951: The O. Henry Awards.* Ed. Herschel Brickell. Garden City, New York: Doubleday, 1951, pp. 299-311.

Rpt. *Short Story Masterpieces.* Ed. Robert Penn Warren and Albert Erskine. New York: Laurel, 1954, pp. 440-54.

Rpt. *Short Stories: A Study in Pleasure.* Ed. Sean O'Faolain. Boston: Little, Brown, 1961, pp. 222-34.

Rpt. *Twenty-Nine Stories.* Ed. William Peden. 2nd ed. Boston: Houghton Mifflin, 1967, pp. 315-27.

Rpt. *Fifty Years of the American Short Story: From the O. Henry Awards, 1919-1970.* Ed. William Abrahams. Vol. II. Garden City, New York: Doubleday, 1970, pp. 289-300.

Rpt. *Women & Men, Men & Women: An Anthology of Short Stories.* Ed. William Smart. New York: St. Martin's, 1975, pp. 363-73.

Rpt. *Initiation: Stories and Short Novels on Three Themes.* Ed. David Thorburn. 2nd ed. New York: Harcourt, 1976, pp. 229-38.

B21 "The Maiden." *New Yorker*, 26 (29 July 1950), 21-25.

In *CABS*, pp. 86-102; *SS*, pp. 51-59; *CS*, pp. 55-64.

B22 "Old Flaming Youth." *Harper's Bazaar*, 84 (Dec. 1950), 94, 182-84, 188.

B23 "The Echo and the Nemesis." (Originally published as "The Nemesis.") *New Yorker*, 26 (16 Dec. 1950), 28-35.

In *CABS*, pp. 10-39; *SS*, pp. 9-25; *CS*, pp. 35-53.

Rpt. *The Best American Short Stories, 1951.* Ed. Martha Foley. Boston: Houghton Mifflin, 1951, pp. 295-311.

Rpt. *Stories, British and American.* Ed. Jack Barry Ludwig and W. Richard Poirier. Boston: Houghton Mifflin, 1953, pp. 398-415.

Rpt. *Sometimes Magic: A Collection of Outstanding Stories for the Teenage Girl.* Ed. Hallie Burnett. New York: Platt & Munk, 1966, pp. 19-41.

Rpt. *Fables of Wit and Elegance.* Ed. Louis Auchincloss. New York: Charles Scribner's, 1972, pp. 192-210.

Rpt. *Travelers: Stories of Americans Abroad.* Ed. L.M. Schulman. New York: Macmillan, 1972, pp. 21-44.

Rpt. *Fat.* Coll. by Kit Reed. Indianapolis: Bobbs Merrill, 1974, pp. 40-60.

1951

B24 "The Healthiest Girl in Town." *New Yorker*, 27 (7 April 1951), 32-40.

In *CS*, pp. 197-217.

Rpt. *The Best American Short Stories, 1952.* Ed. Martha Foley. Boston: Houghton Mifflin, 1952, pp. 271-88.

1952

B25   "The Violet Rock." *New Yorker,* 28 (26 April 1952), 34-42.

B26   "Life Is No Abyss." *Sewanee Review,* 60 (July 1952), 465-87.

In *CS,* pp. 93-112.

B27   "I Love Someone." *Colorado Quarterly,* 1 (Summer 1952), 78-85.

In *CS,* pp. 415-22.

Rpt. *Solo: Women on Women Alone.* Ed. Linda Hamalian and Leo Hamalian. New York: Delacorte, 1977, pp. 186-93.

B28   "The Connoisseurs." *Harper's Bazaar,* 86 (Oct. 1952), 198, 232, 234, 240, 246.

1953

B29   "Cops and Robbers." (Originally published as "The Shorn Lamb.") *New Yorker,* 28 (24 Jan. 1953), 28-34.

In *BC,* pp. 117-34; *SS,* pp. 154-64; *CS,* pp. 423-35.

Rpt. *Prize Stories, 1954: The O. Henry Awards.* Ed. Paul Engle and Hansford Martin. Garden City, New York: Doubleday, 1954, pp. 216-27.

Rpt. *The Best American Short Stories, 1954.* Ed. Martha Foley. Boston: Houghton Mifflin, 1954, pp. 293-305.

B30   "The Liberation." *New Yorker,* 29 (30 May 1953), 22-30; *Perspectives USA,* Summer 1954, pp. 36-54.

In *S,* pp. 3-22; *BC,* pp. 135-59; *SS,* pp. 165-80; *CS,* pp. 305-22.

Rpt. *Love Stories.* Sel. Martin Levin. New York: Quadrangle, 1975, pp. 303-16.

B31 "In the Zoo." *New Yorker*, 29 (19 Sept. 1953), 24-32.

In *S*, pp. 23-45; *BC*, pp. 3-30; *CS*, pp. 283-303.

Rpt. *Prize Stories, 1955: The O. Henry Awards*. Eds. Paul Engle and Hansford Martin. Garden City, New York: Doubleday, 1955, pp. 15-34. (First Prize Story.)

Rpt. *First Prize Stories, 1919-1957: From the O. Henry Memorial Awards*. Garden City, New York: Doubleday, 1957, pp. 496-512.

Rpt. *Stories from the New Yorker, 1950-1960*. New York: Simon & Schuster, 1960, pp. 596-615.

Rpt. *Midland: Twenty-Five Years of Fiction and Poetry Selected from the Writing Workshops of the State University of Iowa*. Ed. Paul Engle. New York: Random, 1961, pp. 261-84.

Rpt. *First Prize Stories, 1919-1963: From the O. Henry Memorial Awards*. Garden City, New York: Doubleday, 1966, pp. 496-512.

Rpt. *Fifty Years of the American Short Story: From the O. Henry Awards*, 1919-1970. Ed. William Abrahams. Vol. II. Garden City, New York: Doubleday, 1970, pp. 301-19.

Rpt. *Story: An Introduction to Prose Fiction*. Ed. Arthur Foff and Daniel Knapp. Belmont, California: Wadsworth, 1964, pp. 299-315.

Rpt. *Scenes from American Life: Contemporary Short Fiction*. Ed. Joyce Carol Oates. New York: Random, 1973, pp. 151-68.

Rpt. *The Norton Anthology of Short Fiction*. Ed. R.V. Cassill. New York: Norton, 1978; 2nd ed., 1981, pp. 1309-25.

1954

B32 "A Winter's Tale." In *New Short Novels* (by Jean Stafford, Elizabeth Etnier, Shelby Foote, and Clyde Miller). Vol. I. Ed. Mary Louise Aswell. New York: Ballantine, 1954.

See A4.

B33   "Bad Characters." *New Yorker,* 30 (4 Dec. 1954), 42-51.

      In *S,* pp. 46-67; *BC,* pp. 3-30; *SS,* pp. 101-18; *CS,* pp. 263-82.

      Rpt. *Points of View: An Anthology of Short Stories.* Ed. James Moffett and Kenneth McElheny. New York: Signet, 1956, pp. 232-51.

      Rpt. *Mid-Century: An Anthology of Distinguished Contemporary American Short Stories.* Comp. Orville Prescott. New York: Washington Square, 1958, pp. 260-80.

      Rpt. *Insight: Literature of Imagination.* Ed. Erwin R. Steinberg et al. New York: Noble, 1969, pp. 34-52.

      Rpt. *The Loners: Short Stories About the Young Alienated.* Ed. L.M. Schulman. New York: Macmillan, 1970, pp. 33-58.

                                1955

B34   "Beatrice Trueblood's Story." *New Yorker,* 31 (26 Feb. 1955), 24-32.

      In *S,* pp. 68-98; *SS,* pp. 238-55; *CS,* pp. 385-405.

      Rpt. *Prize Stories, 1956: The O. Henry Awards.* Ed. Paul Engle and Hansford Martin. Garden City, New York: Doubleday, 1956, pp. 237-57.

      Rpt. *The Experience of the American Woman.* Ed. Barbara H. Solomon. New York: New American, 1978, pp. 252-70.

B35   "Maggie Meriwether's Rich Experience." *New Yorker,* 31 (25 June 1955), 24-30.

      In *S,* pp. 90-108; *CS,* pp. 3-17.

B36   "The Warlock." *New Yorker,* 31 (24 Dec. 1955), 25-28, 30-45.

      Rpt. *Prize Stories, 1957: The O. Henry Awards.* Ed. Paul Engle. Garden City, New York: Doubleday, 1957, pp. 83-106.

Rpt. *Sisters of Sorcery: Two Centuries of Witchcraft Stories by the Gentle Sex.* Ed. Seon Manley and Gogo Lewis. New York: Lothrop, 1976, pp. 73-104.

1956

B37   "The End of a Career." *New Yorker*, 31 (21 Jan. 1956), 35-42.

In *BC*, pp. 31-54; *SS*, pp. 119-33; *CS*, pp. 447-63.

B38   "Caveat Emptor." (Originally published as "The Matchmakers.") *Mademoiselle*, 43 (May 1956), 116, 166-73.

In *BC*, pp. 203-24; *SS*, pp. 189-203; *CS*, pp. 75-90.

Rpt. *Forty Best Stories from* Mademoiselle, *1935-1960.* Ed. Cyrilly Abels and Margarita G. Smith. New York: Harper & Row, 1960, pp. 312-32.

B39   "A Reading Problem." *New Yorker*, 31 (30 June 1956), 24-32.

In *BC*, pp. 173-202; *CS*, pp. 323-44.

B40   "The Mountain Day." *New Yorker*, 32 (18 Aug. 1956), 24-32.

In *CS*, pp. 231-49.

1957

B41   "My Blithe, Sad Bird." *New Yorker*, 33 (6 April 1957), 25-38.

Rpt. *Prize Stories, 1958: The O. Henry Awards.* Ed. Paul Engle and Curtis Harnack. Garden City, New York: Doubleday, 1958, pp. 79-97.

B42   "A Reasonable Facsimile." *New Yorker*, 33 (3 Aug. 1957), 20-30.

In *BC*, pp. 55-87; *SS*, pp. 134-53.

Rpt. *The Best American Short Stories, 1958.* Ed. Martha Foley and David Burnett. Boston: Houghton Mifflin, 1958, pp. 259-80.

Rpt. *Prize Stories, 1959: The O. Henry Awards.* Ed.
Paul Engle. Garden City, New York: Doubleday, 1959,
pp. 105-28.

1958

B43   "The Children's Game." (Originally published as "The
Reluctant Gambler.") *Saturday Evening Post,* 231 (4
Oct. 1958), 35, 90-92, 94.

In *CS,* pp. 19-33.

1959

B44   "The Scarlet Letter." *Mademoiselle,* 49 (July 1959),
62-68, 100-01.

Rpt. *Ten Modern American Short Stories.* Ed. David A.
Sohn. New York: Bantam, 1965, pp. 32-53.

1964

B45   "The Ordeal of Conrad Pardee." *Ladies' Home Journal,*
81 (July 1964), 59, 78, 80-83.

B46   "The Tea Time of Stouthearted Ladies." *Kenyon Review*
(Winter 1964), 116-28.

In *CS,* pp. 219-30.

Rpt. *The Best American Short Stories, 1965.* Ed. Martha
Foley. Boston: Houghton Mifflin, 1965, pp. 313-24.

1968

B47   "The Philosophy Lesson." *New Yorker,* 44 (16 Nov.
1968), 59-63.

In *CS,* pp. 361-69.

1978

B48   "An Influx of Poets." *New Yorker,* 54 (6 Nov. 1978),
43-60.

Extracted from Stafford's unfinished novel, *The
Parliament of Women.* See F60.

Rpt. *Prize Stories, 1980: The O. Henry Awards.* Ed.
William Abrahams. Garden City, New York: Doubleday,
1980, pp. 423-37.

1979

B49   "Woden's Day." *Shenandoah,* 30 (Autumn 1979), 6-26.

Extracted from Stafford's unfinished novel, *The
Parliament of Women.* See F60.

SECTION C

ARTICLES AND ESSAYS

This section lists Jean Stafford's articles and essays, in chronological order, according to the date of their first publication. Information on any later reprintings is also given. Some of Stafford's book reviews could have been included here (see D3, D76, D82, and D85) but, for ease of classification, they have been placed in Section D.

C1   "The Psychological Novel."   *Kenyon Review*, 10 (Spring
1948), 214-27.

In this paper, read at the Bard College *Conference on
the Novel*, Stafford calls "the psychological novel" a
tautology "because the novel does not exist that is not
psychological." While she acknowledges the novelist's
debt to Freud, she denies that he discovered anything
new, arguing that we must not forget "that Shakespeare
knew as much about people as Freud did and that he said
it all very much better."
    She goes on to inveigh against the best-sellers
advertised as "important social documents," "scathing
indictments," and "fearless exposés," arguing that
writers "are not doctors, whose task is to cure, nor
are we courts of law whose task is to condemn. If we
assume either of these roles and are wanting in irony
and are the servants of our pride and prejudice rather
than our sense and sensibility, we may bog down in
self-pity or we may distort our personal misfortune
into polemic or our idiosyncrasy into gospel."
    The problem that faces today's writer, she says, "is
not different from that of serious writers at any other
time in history, and this is true even in spite of the
atomic bomb. For the problem is how to tell the story
so persuasively and vividly that our readers are taken
in and are made to believe that the tale is true, that
these events have happened and could happen again and
do happen everywhere and all the time." This was the
problem of Dostoievsky, Jane Austen, and Flaubert, who
"like all good psychologists ... remain impartial and
do not sit in moral judgment upon their created people
but allow the reader to draw his own conclusions."

C2   "Profiles: American Town."   *New Yorker*, 24 (28 Aug.
1948), 26-30, 35-37.

Tells of her first visit to Newport at the high point
of the summer season.

1949

C3   "Letter from Edinburgh."   *New Yorker*, 25 (17 Sept.
     1949), 83-88.

An account of her attendance at the International
Festival of Music and Drama in Edinburgh.

C4   "Letter from Germany." *New Yorker*, 25 (3 Dec. 1949),
     69-81.

Describes Germany after the war, with special focus on
Nuremberg and Heidelberg. She compares the war-ravaged
country with the Germany she knew before the war.

1951

C5   "Truth and the Novelist." *Harper's Bazaar*, 85 (Aug.
     1951), 139, 187-89; rpt. *Explorations: Reading,
     Thinking, Discussion, Writing.*   Ed. Thomas Clark
     Pollock et al.   Englewood Cliffs, New Jersey:
     Prentice-Hall, 1956, pp. 169-78.

While she acknowledges that all writing is to some
extent autobiographical, she counsels the beginning
writer "to winnow carefully and to add a good portion
of lies, the bigger the better." Early in her career,
she showed some of her work to Ford Madox Ford, who
warned her against writing too directly out of her own
life.   Nevertheless, she then spent three and a half
years trying to write a novel about an experience she
had had in college. Because she felt she had to tell
the truth and nothing but the truth, she could not
bring the story to life, and one day burnt every page
of the twenty-pound manuscript.   This experience
finally convinced her that "too great an addiction to
truth is a hindrance to a writer." (See C11.)

1952

C6   "The Art of Accepting Oneself." *Vogue*, 119 (1 Feb.
     1952), 174-75, 242; rpt. *The Arts of Living: From the
     Pages of* Vogue.   Ed. Ernest Dimnet et al.   New York:
     Simon & Schuster, 1954, pp. 54-62.

Analyzes the conflict between her two minds: Mind A, the reformer, and Mind B, the performer, concluding that "one must accept the warriors and the warriors must accept each other." Such self-acceptance is necessary for loving and lovableness. When the raptures of romantic love have subsided, the mature attitude of the woman toward her lover is one of tolerance. The woman who would have a successful relationship must say, "I do not like these things in him because their counterparts in me are different, but I will accept them for the sake of the whole man. I will neither try to alter the landscape nor to acquire protective coloring, but I will learn the regions that are inimical to me and will avoid them."

1954

C7 "New England Winter." *Holiday*, 15 (Feb. 1954), pp. 34-36; rpt. *Ten Years of* Holiday. New York: Simon & Schuster, 1956, pp. 340-47; excerpt. *Holiday*, 57 (March 1976), 28, 65.

An evocation of the beauties of the New England winter, especially as experienced in Damariscotta Mills, Maine, where she and Lowell lived for awhile. (This locale provided the setting for *CW* and for several of her short stories.)

1960

C8 "Souvenirs of Survival: The Thirties Revisited." *Mademoiselle*, 50 (Feb. 1960), 90-91, 174-76.

Writes of her experiences at the University of Colorado during the Great Depression and of her year in Nazi Germany at the University of Heidelberg. She and a classmate recently talked over those days: "We said that people these days were afraid of getting their hearts broken and how, we asked each other, can you function fully unless your heart has been broken about a thousand times before you reach the age of franchise? Broken by cooled-off lovers, but broken also by causes that turned into jokes and heroes whose feet lost their wings and became clay. Our romantic vanity over the scars of our hearts is, I daresay, as bootless as the vanity of a German student corpsman

over the signature of duels of honor on his face, but
we cherish the souvenirs of our survival."

1962

C9   "Shahrazad's   Tales: An   Introduction   by   Jean
     Stafford." *Arabian Nights: The Lion and the Carpenter
     and Other Tales from the Arabian Nights Retold.* New
     York: Macmillan, 1962, pp. iii-iv.

     Recounts the story of Shahrazad and gives a brief
     history of *The Arabian Nights Entertainments.*

1965

C10 "The Strange World of Marguerite Oswald." *McCall's,* 93
     (Oct. 1965), 112-113, 192-194, 196-200, 202.

     Based on Stafford's three days of interviews with Mrs.
     Oswald.   This article was later reprinted as a large
     part of *A Mother in History.* (See A14, G158-86, and
     H63.)

1966

C11 "Truth in Fiction." *Library Journal,* 91 (1 Oct. 1966),
     4557-65.

     Contains much of the same material as "Truth and the
     Novelist" (C5).   In addition, however, Stafford
     includes a reminiscence of her friendship with Sax
     Rohmer, the creater of Fu Manchu, in New York in the
     late forties. She also talks about her experiences in
     writing *A Mother in History.*

1968

C12 "To School with Joy." *Vogue,* 151 (May 1968), 258-61,
     128.

     Article on Mrs. Warren G. Topping and on the Hampton
     Day School in Long Island, which Topping founded in
     1966.

1970

C13 "My (Ugh!) Sensitivity Training." *Horizon,* 12 (Spring
     1970), 112.

Stafford's indignant account of her experience as a "trainee" in a "sensitivity training group," in which a magazine asked her to take part. She includes the letter she sent to the sponsor of this group, expressing her outrage over such attempts "to debase a once respectable discipline, that of psychology, to the level of the shell game."

C14 "Love Among the Rattlesnakes." *McCall's*, 97 (March 1970), 68-69, 145-46.

Stafford tries to puzzle out why the Tate murders happened. After pointing out the similarities between Manson's cult and the practices of the Assassins active in Persia and Syria in the eleventh and twelfth centuries, she goes on to consider the reasons for Manson's popularity among his women followers. The major reason was perhaps that they had been "unacquainted with familial love." Their willingness to call themselves "Manson's slaves" suggests that "the emancipation of women has so far fallen from its ideal that women no longer want it." In spite of their heinous crimes, Stafford feels that the girls deserve compassion "as members of a criminally permissive (ergo, *neglectful*) society."

1971

C15 "Introduction." *The American Coast.* New York: Charles Scribner's, 1971, 15-27.

Stafford begins with some comments on the philosophical significance of the sea: not the least of the sea's enticements is its "very supreme, capricious disregard for human life and human endeavor. The contemplation of the sea and of the firmament it mirrors is the closest we can come to a study of eternal time and infinite space." Then, after a brief autobiographical reminiscence of the beaches of Southern California, the first beaches she knew, she dwells at length on the enchantments of the Long Island coastline.

C16 "The Unexpected Joys of a Simple Garden." *Redbook*, 137 (June 1971), 79, 179-80.

On the gardens she has tended and enjoyed.

C17   "Suffering Summer Houseguests." *Vogue*, 158 (15 Aug.
      1971), 112.

      Gives the hostess some suggestions for furnishing the
      guest room.

C18   "Intimations   of   Hope."   *McCall's*, 99 (Dec. 1971), 77,
      118, 120.

      One cause for Stafford's intimations of hope at this
      Christmas season is that the "hordes of Dumb Doras and
      Xanthippes and common scolds" who joined the women's
      liberation movement in the beginning "seem lately to
      have piped down, maybe run out of gas, and studious
      women, like studious students, have awakened to their
      responsibilities, as well as to their rights and
      privileges." Furthermore, the "aggressive apathy" of
      students, which she encountered a few years ago as a
      teacher and lecturer, "is giving way, and the energetic
      aspiration to learn and to understand is returning to
      campuses."

C19   "East Hampton from the Catbird Seat." New York *Times*,
      26 Dec. 1971, Sec. 1A, pp. 1, 13.

      An idyllic sketch of her life in East Hampton, Long
      Island, in A.J. Liebling's house, where Stafford lived
      year-round after his death. In this piece she vows to
      quit "my dwelling in my hamlet only for my grave, a
      mile and a half away." (Eight years later, Stafford was
      buried in this grave, beside Liebling's.)

                              1972

C20   "What Does Martha Mitchell Know?" *McCall's*, 100 (Oct.
      1972), 8, 10, 28, 31, 120.

      Describes the background of Martha Mitchell and her
      life as an important Washington wife, and speculates on
      the reasons for her current and uncharacteristic
      silence. Stafford also includes a reminiscence of her
      own experience as a teacher at Stephens College in
      Columbia, Missouri, which Martha (Beall) Mitchell
      attended for a year.

1973

C21 "Don't Send Me Gladiolus." *Vogue*, 161 (March 1973), 146.

Asking her readers to remember that "Sickness is a condition; and is not a social occasion," Stafford gives some rules she would like her hospital visitors to observe; the first group of rules relate to the handling of visits, the second group to the kinds of gifts to bring.

C22 "Don't Use Ms. with Miss Stafford, Unless You Mean ms." New York *Times*, 21 Sept. 1973, p. 36.

When Stafford receives a letter addressed to her as Ms., she circles the "Ms." in red and writes on the envelope: "Not acceptable to addressee. Return to sender." She argues that since she is not a manuscript or a Master of Science, and does not have multiple sclerosis, a motorship, a mail steamer, etc., the title is meaningless. She also pokes fun at the genderless nouns and pronouns.

C23 "On My Mind." *Vogue*, 162 (Nov. 1973), 200-01, 250, 254.

Comments on the gifts she has given and received throughout her life; she draws up some rules for gift-giving, summarizing them all with "Don't Be Stupid, and Have a Heart."

C24 "Katharine Graham." *Vogue*, 162 (Dec. 1973), 202-05, 218-19, 221.

A highly complimentary article about the press, as well as about Katharine Graham, publisher of the Washington (D.C.) *Post*.

C25 "Plight of the American Language." *Saturday Review World*, 1 (4 Dec. 1973), 14-18.

Inveighs against the neologisms, solecisms, "mongloid bastards," "knock-kneed metaphors," jargon, and gibberish, which she sees to be characteristic of present-day American English. "The prognosis for the ailing language is not good. I predict that it will

not die in my lifetime, but I fear that it will be
assailed by countless cerebral accidents and massive
strokes and gross insults to the brain and finally will
no longer be able to sit up in bed and take nourishment
by mouth."

1974

C26   "Contagious Imbecibility." *New York Times Book Review*,
       5 May 1974, pp. 8-12.

       Stafford lets off steam about a number of things, from
       bank tellers in miniskirts who chew gum, to being able
       to "buy only an imitation liquid soap that lay on top
       of our hard water like a membrane penetrable only by
       ice pick," but the chief cause of her state of
       indignation here is the advertising campaign being
       conducted by the National Book Committee and the
       American Library Association, marking National Library
       Week. She takes particular exception to their posters
       which read, "YOU'VE GOT A RIGHT TO READ. DON'T BLOW
       IT."

C27   "Modern Romanticism: Lally Weymouth." *Vogue*, 163 (June
       1974), 86, 145.

       Portrait of Lally Weymouth, daughter of Katharine
       Graham of the Washington (D.C.) *Post*.

C28   "Once upon a time, Con Edison made a big mistake in
       Jean Stafford's gas bill. Well, she's a writer and
       relishes a good fight. But wait, let her tell it in
       her own words." New York *Times*, 8 June 1974, p. 31.

       A report on her confrontation with New York's
       Consolidated Edison over an erroneous bill. She gives
       details about the letters, beginning with a seven-page
       one, she wrote to the officials of the company, as well
       as about the numerous telephone calls which followed.
       The saga ended with Con Ed's refund to Stafford for 23
       cents.

C29   "Wordman, Spare That Tree!" *Saturday Review World*, 1
       (13 July 1974), 14-17.

       Too many books are being published today because of
       publishers' desires for money. "It occurs to me with

woe and rage that thousands and thousands of trees are
being chopped down right now and being made into pulp
and the pulp made into paper on which will be written
hundreds of worthless and rottenly written books about
why we must stop cutting down our trees."

C30 "Somebody Out There Hates Me." *Esquire*, 82 (Aug.
1974), 108-09.

Speaks of the large quantity of hate mail she has
received. In response to her essay on why she disliked
being addressed as "Ms." (C22), many accused her of
being flippant about the feminist movement. "The fact
is," Stafford says, "that I don't give a hang about the
movement one way or another." Also, after her
interviews with Mrs. Oswald appeared in *McCall's* (C10),
she was "inundated by an avalanche of hate mail so
impassioned and so various that I went quite funny in
the head and took to wearing a false nose and a
peculiar hat when I went to the supermarket or the
hardware store." She understands why she receives
these letters: "The venting of spleen and bile is
relieving and, if it offends and is sourly returned,
perversely delicious!"

C31 "Some Advice to Hostesses from a Well-Tempered
Guest." *Vogue*, 164 (Sept. 1974), 296-98.

Beginning with a reminiscence of her mother's childhood
memory book, Stafford goes on to give pointers on how
to handle modern dinner parties correctly, for both
hostesses and guests. She gives the details of a few
disastrous dinner parties she has known.

C32 "At This Point in Time, TV Is Murdering the English
Language." New York *Times*, 15 Sept. 1974, Sec. II, pp.
23, 27.

Gives numerous examples to support her thesis that "The
high linguistic crimes committed by television's
newscasters and advertisers have impoverished the
richest language in the world."

C33 "The Crossword Puzzle Has Gone to Hell!" *Esquire*, 82
(Dec. 1974), 144-45.

Tells of her life-long love of working crossword puzzles, but the presence of "many offensive linguistic and orthographic habits" in modern crossword puzzles has caused her to give up the practice.

1975

C34   "On Books to Read Before Sleep." *Mademoiselle*, 81 (Feb. 1975), 154, 156, 159.

Comments on the books that she keeps by her bedside: *The Complete Works of Lewis Carroll*, *The Complete Short Stories of Robert Louis Stevenson*, Eudora Welty's *A Curtain of Green* and *The Ponder Heart* (though she is delighted by just about "every word Eudora Welty puts on paper"), *The Collected Stories of Peter Taylor*, a volume of Ring Lardner stories, *The Pillow Book of Sei Shonagon*, and Joseph Mitchell's *McSorley's Wonderful Saloon*.

C35   "Why I Don't Get Around Much Anymore." *Esquire*, 83 (March 1975), 114, 132, 134.

In this humorous article, Stafford gives the details of several of her trips, the onerousness of which has led her to vow that "If I ever go farther than six miles from home, it will be by ambulance and I will be under general anesthetic."

C36   "Millicent Fenwick Makes an Adroit Politician." *Vogue*, 165 (June 1975), 120-21, 139-40.

An admiring portrait of Millicent Fenwick, Republican, U.S. Representative from the Fifth Congressional District of New Jersey. Stafford feels that the aristocratic Fenwick well satisfies the American need, "in times of distress, to look for help among the founding fathers."

C37   "Introduction." *The Press* by A.J. Liebling. 2nd rev. ed. New York: Ballantine, 1975, pp. ix-xiii.

Recounts A.J. Liebling's life-long love of the press, calling it "his wayward concubine."

C38   "Coca-Cola." *Esquire*, 84 (Dec. 1975), 96, 178-79.

Relates several experiences she has had with Coca-Cola from the time she first tasted it as a child up to the present. In recent years, she has been dismayed by the substitution of aluminum cans for the green glass returnable bottles. Once, when she found a completely empty can among the eight-pack she had bought, she wrote a letter of complaint to the public relations department of the New York branch. The result was that two young men came to her door, bringing "the heartfelt apologies of Management" and "two wooden cases of green, glass, six-and-a-half-ounce bottles of The Real Thing."

1976

C39   "Heroes and Villains: Who Was Famous and Why." *McCall's*, 103 (April 1976), 196-99, 265-67, 270.

Comments on the many American heroes and a few of the villains who have peopled American history, beginning with General Custer and Wild Bill Hickock (who were really, as she points out, villains). And, although today "we have had bumper crops of Mephistophelian murderers and thieves and traitors," modern boredom, and a high threshold for shock, and terror deprive us of "real villains to boo and hiss at. You have a bunch of punks."

C40   "Miss McKeehan's Pocketbook." *Colorado Quarterly*, 24 (Spring 1976), 407-11.

An autobiographical reminiscence prompted by finding in her attic an old pocketbook which she had bought years ago because it reminded her of the one carried by Miss McKeehan, one of her favorite teachers at the University of Colorado, and as a result of whose influence Stafford began her thirty-year career as a writer. Stafford concludes the essay by saying that she is gradually accumulating a collection of essays, reviews, lectures, and "angry letters to public utility companies that I have written over the years, and I intend to call this omnium-gatherum 'Miss McKeehan's Pocketbook.'"

SECTION D

REVIEWS BY STAFFORD

This section lists Jean Stafford's book and movie reviews. The entries are arranged in chronological order. Information on all later reprintings is also given.

D1   "Walpurgis Nacht, 1940."   *Kenyon Review*, 4 (Winter 1942), 106-08.

Rev. of *The Journal of Albion Moonlight* by Kenneth Patchen.

Signed "Jean Stafford Lowell."

"If Mr. Patchen really believes the world to be as rotten as he intimates, then he is operating on carrion, and the performance is neither dextrous nor fragrant."

1944

D2   "Empty Net." *Partisan Review*, 11 (Winter 1944), 114-15.

Rev. of *The Wide and Other Stories* by Eudora Welty.

Compares this new book unfavorably with Welty's first volume, *The Curtain of Green.*

1959

D3   "The Eat Generation." *Reporter*, 19 Feb. 1959, pp. 33-34.   Rpt. *Essays Today, 1960.*   Ed. Richard M. Ludwig. New York: Harcourt Brace, 1960, pp. 89-93.

Rev. of *The Fume of Poppies* by Jonathan Kozol.

In this novel, the delight of the protagonists (Wendy and Lamby) in each other is excelled only by their mutual interest in food--just good, wholesome food. By the end of the novel, they are engaged to be married, and Stafford says, "It's my bet that if Wendy hasn't lost her touch with mashed potatoes and pancakes, and if she keeps plenty of milk and cucumbers on hand and meat in the freezer for cookouts on the patio, this marriage will take the cake."

1960

D4   "Rara Avis." *Reporter*, 23 (22 Dec. 1960), 40, 42, 44.

Rev. of *A Lady's Life in the Rocky Mountains* by Isabella L. Bird.

"Isabella Bird had a faithful eye for shape and color, and I know of no other writer who has so well captured the looks and personality of unchanging mountains. She writes magnificently of magnificent skies and royally of royal storms." This is an excellent report on "the restless, changing kaleidoscopic West" during the 1870's.

1961

D5   "The Hindu Trilogy." *Horizon*, 3 (Jan. 1961), 115.

Movie review of Satyajit Ray's *Pather Panchali*, *Aparajito*, and *The World of Apu*.

D6   "Neo-realismo Revisited." *Horizon*, 3 (March 1961), 98-100.

Movie review of Roberto Rossellini's *General Della Rovere* and Vittorio De Sica's *Umberto D.* and *The Gold of Naples*.

D7   "Samurai, With Sword, Won't Travel." *Horizon*, 3 (May 1961), 114-15.

Review of the movie, *The Magnificent Seven*.

1962

D8   "The Works of God, the Ways of Man." *New Republic*, 146 (18 June 1962), 21-22.

Rev. of *The Slave* by Isaac Bashevis Singer.

Singer "is a spell-binder as clever as Scheherazade." Through his "remarkable gifts as a story teller," he keeps "the attention and sympathy of

his reader through a fiction that is a combination
movie scenario and hagiography. It is an admirable
performance."

1964

D9   *Vogue*, 143 (15 Jan. 1964), 27.

Rev. of *The Ragman's Daughter and Other Stories* by
Alan Sillitoe.

Although some of these stories "are anecdotal and
there is an unworthy facility in their resolutions,"
as well as "occasionally a tone that threatens to
become maudlin," the "workmanship and spirit" of the
best of them "are forthright and energetic and the
comedy comes with ease...."

D10 *Vogue*, 143 (15 March 1964), 70.

Rev. of *The Martyred* by Richard E. Kim.

"While Mr. Kim does not write of war as Tolstoi did,
or Stephen Crane, or Hemingway, he earns his laurels
as a writer about war; and although his argument is
moral, he does not sit in judgment and never slides
into preaching cadences. His prose is as clean and
unencumbered as a blade of grass."

D11 "A Sense of the Past." *New York Review of Books*, 2
(19 March 1964), 11-12.

Rev. of *New York Landmarks*, ed. Alan Burnham.

This is "an impressive compilation" of photographs of
New York houses and public buildings which merit
preservation because of their historic meaning or
architectural value.

D12 *Vogue*, 143 (15 April 1964), 56.

Rev. of *My Heart Is Broken* by Mavis Gallant.

"There are degrees of excellence in this book, but it
is always good. Miss Gallant's gift is very feminine
and very sinewy. Her prose is prepossessing."

D13   *Vogue*, 143 (May 1964), 61.

    Rev. of *The Plant, the Well, the Angel* by Vassilis Vassilikos.

    "Vassilikos' originality lies in the ability of his sharp-eyed, ironic Greek intelligence to clothe Man and his habitat in modern dress but not to disturb the patina of antiquity. He has read Kafka surely, but he took in the ancient mysteries with his mother's milk."

D14   *Vogue*, 144 (July 1964), 32.

    Rev. of *The Soul of Kindness* by Elizabeth Taylor.

    "Mrs. Taylor writes, as she has always done, about people unmemorable save in their relationships to one another; she completely knows her cast and she writes with a perfect poise and an adroitly embedded wit."

D15   *Vogue*, 144 (15 Aug. 1964), 39.

    Rev. of *Scented Gardens for the Blind* by Janet Frame.

    This "untidy" book is not so much a novel as it is "a symposium of three monologists whose assignment is a free-style investigation into Life, Death, and kindred matters."

    Rev. of *Letters from Bohemia* by Ben Hecht.

    If Hecht's recollections of his seven friends "are founded in fact, it would be hard to assemble a more bad-mannered, tasteless, criminally sentimental, boastful pack of windbags...."

D16   "Living Through the War." *New York Review of Books*, 3 (10 Sept. 1964), 15-16.

    Rev. of *Divided Loyalties* by J.T. du Cros.

    Stafford mainly describes the content of this book, the account of a Scotswoman living in Occupied France during World War II.

D17   *Vogue*, 144 (15 Sept. 1964), 78.

Rev. of *The Offensive Traveller* by V.S. Pritchett.

Pritchett is "surely one of the most ingratiating of living writers." His prose in this collection of travel essays "is as warm and clear as sunlight."

D18   *Vogue*, 144 (1 Oct. 1964), 108.

Rev. of *Charles Chaplin: My Autobiography*.

"Unfortunately, the genius of this greatest of clowns does not shine through the murk of verbiage and ill-will, and what should have been one of the most interesting books of our time, is the most disappointing."

D19   *Vogue*, 144 (15 Oct. 1964), 98.

Rev. of *The Words* by Jean-Paul Sartre.

Sartre's autobiography is disappointing because unrevealing: "It is not that one finishes *The Words* without multitudinous impressions and admiring recollections of stunningly clever feats of legerdemain, and stars of wit, and glades of charm, but that essentially one has been made a fool of in a game of hide-and-seek with an adversary who is a much bigger boy."

D20   *Vogue*, 144 (1 Nov. 1964), 78.

Rev. of *Herzog* by Saul Bellow.

This novel "is a work of elegance. It is wrought elaborately in several laminations, and every article of its ornamentation is resistant to sentimentality, or vulgarity, or irrelevance."

Rev. of *Vive Moi!* by Sean O'Faolin.

Much of this autobiography is "cerebral and circumlocutory and fuzzy."

D21   *Vogue*, 144 (Dec. 1964), 148.

       Rev. of *Cabot Wright Begins* by James Purdy.

       This novel is "a joke, well told in several dialects--
       Wall Street, Madison Avenue, the Bedchamber--and at
       times it achieves a splendour of dementia," but it is
       "too long."

                                1965

D22   *Vogue*, 145 (1 Jan. 1965), 67.

       Rev. of *Astrology* by Louis MacNeice.

       "Perhaps to the aficionado, this miscellany will be
       entertaining and practical. To others there will seem
       to be too much rice pudding for the raisins."

D23   *Vogue*, 145 (1 Feb. 1965), 97.

       Rev. of *The Door in the Wall* by Oliver La Farge.

       "These stories are not profound but they are agreeably
       readable, and clearly the man who wrote them wore his
       learning gracefully."

D24   "The Collector." *New York Review of Books*, 5 (14 Oct.
       1965), 12-14.

       Rev. of *Mrs. Jack* by Louise Hall Tharp.

       In this "exasperating" book, Tharp "tends to pussy-
       foot around her anecdotes, archly pulling her punches,
       or to gush them out, putting her exclamation marks in
       the   wrong   places."   Nevertheless,   it   is   good
       entertainment: "one likes to read about paradoxes and
       one likes to read about the very rich at play, buying
       whatever takes their fancy--the silks and precious
       gems of Cathay, the specialty of the moment in
       Samarkand, the pretty old pictures in funny old
       palaces in Italy--particularly when what takes their
       fancy is the genuine article."

D25   "This Happy Breed." *New York Review of Books*, 5 (23
       Dec. 1965), 14.

Rev. of *The Gentle Americans* by Helen Howe.

This nostalgic book about the Bostonian aristocracy "calls forth helpless yearnings for time intransigently past."

1966

D26 *Vogue*, 147 (1 Jan. 1966), 71.

Rev. of *Doobie Doo* by Ivan C. Karp ("awfully funny"), *The Evening of the Holiday* by Shirley Hazzard ("graceful and, though it is studious, it lacks earnestness"), and *After Julius* by Elizabeth Jane Howard ("virtuoso writing").

D27 *Vogue*, 147 (15 Jan. 1966), 35.

Rev. of *In Cold Blood* by Truman Capote.

This "extraordinarily perceived and brilliantly executed new book," is "more than a study of a specific crime and an exhaustive examination of the criminals who perpetrated it. It is a sounding of the depthless evil existing in the sub-strata of society and a clear-eyed look at the eruptions ot it into violence, eruptions that now have reached the point of epidemic."

D28 *Vogue*, 147 (15 Feb. 1966), 57.

Rev. of *Aldous Huxley*, ed. Julian Huxley.

This is "an astute evaluation of one of the most interesting figures of our time and an engrossing revelation of a cordial, witty, civilized man."

Rev. of *The Comedians* by Graham Greene.

The book is "full of taint and prurience, and no matter what one's persuasion, one wishes Greene would leave the Church out of it."

D29 *Vogue*, 147 (15 March 1966), 60.

Rev. of *My Brother Brendan* by Dominic Behan ("a pointless memoir"), *The Beginners* by Dan Jacobson

("the non-work of an able writer who is slackly
lounging about"), and *Toddler on the Run* by Shena
Mackay ("an easy book to while away the time--that is,
about half an hour").

D30   *Vogue*, 147 (June 1966), 55.

Rev. of *The Case of Mr. Crump* by Ludwig Lewisohn.

Stafford read this novel "at one gulp," finding herself "alive with suspense, revolted at the kind of
evil that is laid bare here."

D31   *Vogue*, 148 (1 Aug. 1966), 58.

Rev. of *The Last Gentleman* by Walker Percy.

"The moral of this brilliantly comic and serious
adventure is: 'Lucky is the man who does not secretly
believe that every possibility is open to him.'"

D32   *Vogue*, 148 (15 Sept. 1966), 75.

Rev. of *The Pilgrim Hawk* by Glenway Wescott (this
reissue of the 1940 novella "has lost none of its
merit in the intervening years"), and *Under Gemini* by
Isabel Bolton ("in faultless prose.")

D33   *Vogue*, 148 (15 Oct. 1966), 80.

Rev. of *The Birds Fall Down* by Rebecca West.

"It scarcely seems possible that this inflated and
interminable imbroglio was perpetrated by the same
writer who has reported on treason and other forms of
criminality with acumen, with perception of motive and
character, and with tension."

D34   *Vogue*, 148 (Dec. 1966), 167.

Rev. of *The Territorial Imperative* by Robert Ardrey.

If this "engrossing and often irritating book" is read
"as a compendium of engaging, horrifying, comic
examples of conduct in the natural world, then it is
fascinating; but if it is to be looked on as the
revelation of the ur-ethos, the mind's eye blurs."

1967

D35   *Vogue*, 149 (1 Jan. 1967), 52.

Rev. of *La Maison de Rendez-vous* by Alain Robbe-
Grillet.

"Reading Alain Robbe-Grillet is something like living
through shallow sleep in which, although the dreams
are multitudinous and thronged with incandescent
detail, not one of them can be detained for
examination; rather, they are linked together in a
crude, maddening, strangling concatenation, and one
awakes after such a night exhausted, bad-tempered,
obscurely apprehensive, and depressed.... The
monotonous staccato is finally as irritating as a
dripping water tap."

D36   *Vogue*, 149 (15 Feb. 1967), 63.

Rev. of *When She Was Good* by Philip Roth.

After reading this novel, "One feels that one has
spent a long Thanksgiving day with a hinterland family
whose interests, ambitions, politics, houses,
automobiles, food, and tragedies are so studiously
average that they should be subjects for a
statistician rather than a novelist."

D37   *Vogue*, 149 (15 March 1967), 56.

Rev. of *The Eighth Day* by Thornton Wilder.

This is "a large, richly discursive novel, part murder
mystery, part family saga, part inquiry into human
behaviour.... It is, even at its most disquisitive, a
rattling good yarn."

D38   *Vogue*, 149 (June 1967), 78.

Rev. of *May We Borrow Your Husband* by Graham Greene
("agile and urbane"), and *The Deep End* by Joseph Hayes
(messes "around with morality and values and the
phenomenon of juvenile putrefaction in the modern
world to such an extent that the tensions of his story
sag and at last collapse under a burden of highfalutin
but superficial exposition").

D39   *Vogue*, 150 (15 Aug. 1967), 74.

Rev. of *Signs and Wonders* by Francoise Mallet-Joris.

"Mme. Mallet-Joris ... has a robust and fluent talent that feeds an elaborate reticulum of tributaries: She has the gifts of narrative design, of meditative interpolation that is never didactic and never irrelevant, of Theophrastan portraiture; she can reveal landscapes, interiors, physiognomies, meals, skies quickly and acutely without ever resorting to inventory; she can enter the bedrooms of lovers with the propriety of a misty wind. She is a most womanly writer but she is tailored rather than furbelowed."

D40   *Vogue*, 150 (15 Oct. 1967), 69.

Rev. of *The Other Side* by Alfred Kubin.

"Scene after scene of unspeakable violence and corruption is unfolded before the reader who at last is too surfeited to cringe; he can only turn away, so put upon that he has become indifferent, and say, 'Lawk a mercy on me,/ This is none of I!'"

1968

D41   "Lioness." *New York Review of Books*, 10 (18 Jan. 1968), 19-22.

Rev. of *Titania: The Biography of Isak Dinesen* by Parmenia Migel.

Stafford suggests that the admirers of Isak Dinesen avoid this book: "they will do better to remember her as a lioness than to learn about her as a monkey queen."

D42   *Vogue*, 151 (1 Feb. 1968), 108.

Rev. of *The Day We Got Drunk on Cake* by William Trevor.

In this "uncommonly readable collection" of stories, "Mr. Trevor's wit of eye and ear, his ingenuity of plotting are so very accomplished that one can be seduced into reading these stories as farces.   On second thoughts, however, they are keenly disturbing, bringing one to the realization that a great part of the population, working at jobs, going about freely, exercising the franchise, are certifiably mad but are enclothed in so plausible an integument that they will never attract the attention of the authorities. They do not endanger society but they undermine and harass individual lives."

D43   *Vogue*, 151 (15 March 1968), 46.

Rev. of *Les Belles Images* by Simone de Beauvoir.

"Patrick O'Brian, the translator, may be partly to blame; but one fears that Mlle. de Beauvoir and no one else is responsible for the banality of situation, the inertia of language, the bromidic observations of a stereotyped dramatis personae, and the girlish musings on Broad General Concepts.... This is one of those books that cause men to use the denomination 'woman writer' as an acidulous pejorative.   It is quite literally too silly to be true."

D44   *Vogue*, 151 (1 April 1968), 138.

Rev. of *Tunc* by Lawrence Durrell.

Stafford criticizes Durrell's "gimmicks of diction," his "clutter of eccentricity that impedes the progress of the narrative and the cacophony that rises from it, like the joyful squawks of rats and the exuberant shrieks of scavanger birds," and his "infuriating linguistic attitudinizing."

D45   *Vogue*, 151 (15 April 1968), 44.

Rev. of *Lord Malquist & Mr. Moon* by Tom Stoppard.

"Stoppard's talent as an entertainer is certain and brilliant; his intention as a commentator is less clearly defined so that, although one has had a good time, one is left somewhat up in the air and a little uneasy at the thought of presently being brought to earth with a thud."

D46   "Wolfe Hunting." *New York Review of Books*, 19 (9 May 1968), 17-20.

Rev. of *Thomas Wolfe, a Biography* by Andrew Turnbull, and *The Letters of Thomas Wolfe to His Mother*, ed. C.H. Holman and Sue Fields Ross.

"Although Turnbull's *Biography* is exhaustive and there is no reason to dispute his facts, he is so much in agreement with his subject about his subject's towering genius that for the most part he sounds as if he is writing flap copy for 'The Collected Works of Thomas Wolfe.' The *Letters* are infinitely more revealing; the man therein revealed is infuriating and pathetic, so deformed by self-absorption and self-indulgence, so macerated by his warm bath of self-pity, so worshipful of the physical appetites he deified that he was incapable of deep friendship or deep love or of any but Mother's Day filial piety."

D47   *Vogue*, 152 (15 Aug. 1968), 48.

Rev. of *Lost in the Funhouse* by John Barth.

Barth "presents fictions, ontological lucubrations, Homeric yarns in modern dress, and other works of nomenclature. One wishes one could join in the frolic because the author is having such a walloping good time with his distorting mirrors, ventriloquism, legerdemain, his pyrotechnics that combine girandoles of erudition with waggish pieces in the vernacular. But a good deal of the time one feels hornswoggled."

D48   *Vogue*, 152 (1 Sept. 1968), 270.

Rev. of *Morning Noon and Night* by James Gould Cozzens.

Stafford calls Cozzens, with six of his ten books being Books-of-the-Month Club selections, "the Willie Mays of fictioneers." One of the things she objects to in this novel is the repetition of the name of the narrator, Hank: "you can't imagine how stridently this begins to sound like a fingernail on the blackboard."

D49   *Vogue*, 152 (1 Oct. 1968), 145.

Rev. of *Sears Roebuck Catalogue 1897*.

This is "a sort of Larousse of the costumes and housefurnishings, the amusements, the gastronomic and reading habits of Americans at the turn of the century. To those attached to reference books and to Americana, it is a desideratum if not an absolute necessity."

D50   "Sensations Sweet and Sour." *McCall's*, 96 (Dec. 1968), 24, 114-15.

Review of the movies *Star!*, *Finian's Rainbow*, *The Impossible Years*, *The Bliss of Mrs. Blossom*, and *Hot Millions*.

1969

D51   *Vogue*, 153 (15 March 1969), 40.

Rev. of *A Compass Error* by Sybille Bedford.

"The matters under examination are a case of blameless adultery performed off-stage and revealed through lengthy monologues and a lengthy letter; and Flavia's introduction, at seventeen, to Lesbian love. The fact that one of her two lady-loves is the wife of the adulterer and the fact that the adulteress is Flavia's mother complicate things and provide armature for a plot."

D52   *New York Times Book Review*, 13 April 1969, pp. 4-5.

Rev. of *Naked in Garden Hills* by Harry Crews.

"Macabre and slapstick, howlingly funny and as sad as a zoo, ribald, admonitory, wry and deeply fond."

D53   "Spirits." *New York Review of Books*, 12 (24 April 1969), 26-29.

Rev. of *Being Geniuses Together* by Kay Boyle and Robert McAlmon; *Those Remarkable Cunards, Emerald and Nancy* by Daphne Fielding; and *Nancy Cunard: Brave Poet, Indomitable Rebel*, ed. Hugh Ford.

Stafford gives a mainly biographical account of the lives of Nancy Cunard, Kay Boyle, and Robert McAlmon, based on these three books.

D54   *Vogue*, 153 (June 1969), 64, 66.

      Rev. of *Ada* by Vladimir Nabokov.

      "The plot is as complex as an Elizabethan play or the
      Nibelungenlied but it proceeds, though often doubling
      back, at a great rate; the detail is, indeed,
      charming, arresting, titivating."

D55   *Vogue*, 154 (15 Aug. 1969), 40.

      Rev. of *The Process* by Brion Gysin.

      "As a rule, a want of personal recognition does not
      baffle my appreciation of fiction. I can be airborne
      with the Roc; I can be a cat about Mme. Verdurin's
      parties; Huck Finn's pap, Mrs. Ape, Grendel's mother,
      and Fu Manchu are as familiar to me as my next of
      kin. In the course of my reading life I have under-
      gone childbed, shipwreck, public disgrace, kingship,
      popeship, exile, apoplexy, epilepsy, prostitution, or
      death. But it is not possible, although I wish it
      were, for me to accompany Brion Gysin on a protracted
      kif-trip" in this novel.

D56   *Vogue*, 154 (1 Sept. 1969), 338.

      Rev. of *Come Back If It Doesn't Get Any Better* by
      Penelope Gilliatt.

      All of these stories are "brilliant but some are more
      amazingly so than others. Miss Gilliatt's materials
      are friendship and marriage and the ententes and
      Armageddons within families; frequently the parties to
      these conjugations are eccentric, are close to lunacy,
      and to her teratological examinations and diagnoses
      she brings a rational enlightenment, a serene and
      generous acceptance that make her comic genius soar
      into the empyrean with no sound of motors running."

D57   *New York Times Book Review*, 7 Sept. 1969, p. 53.

      Rev. of *How to Raise a Dog in the City and in the
      Suburbs* by James R. Kinney.

      "Such is his reassuring, no-nonsense authority and
      good humor that if I were a dog, I would doctor with
      him."

D58   *Vogue*, 154 (1 Oct. 1969), 156.

Rev. of *Mile High* by Richard Condon.

This is a "long, improbable, badly written, and
ingenious new novel." Nevertheless, "although Richard
Condon's plotting is often reminiscent of Batman, in
general his material is so engrossing that one does
not put the book down despite the fact that it is
trash."

D59   *Vogue*, 154 (15 Oct. 1969), 58.

Rev. of *The Throwaway Children* by Lisa Aversa
Richette.

Richette "has made a scrupulous and alarming
examination of juvenile delinquency and the emotional
disorders that bring it on; she has made a shocking
report of the slipshod, antiquated, and sometimes
barbarous ways in which the tragic mess is being
handled; and she has made a fervent plea that
something positive and radical be done to save the
children."

D60   "Survivor." *New York Review of Books*, 13 (23 Oct.
1969), 31-32.

Rev. of *Only One Year* by Svetlana Alliluyeva, tr. Paul
Chavchavadze.

Stafford criticizes this autobiographical account of
Stalin's daughter for being "naive, mushy, repetitious, and often nebulous, pious and dull."
Nevertheless, "the guilelessness, the sentimentality,
the reliance on eternal verities, are not only natural
but are, in view of the accident of her birth, necessary and right. And, having come to that conclusion,
I brush aside my complaint that her story is wanting
in immediacy and power and, contemplating the plain
fact of her survival, am impressed."

1970

D61   "Merchants and Masterpieces." *New York Times Book
Review*, 12 April 1970, pp. 8, 42.

Rev. of *The Story of the Metropolitan Museum of Art* by
Calvin Tomkins.

Stafford praises this "big and engrossing book," for
being "generously strewn with well-told anecdotes,
some of them fresh and some of them twice-told tales."

D62   *Vogue*, 155 (15 April 1970), 60.

Rev. of *A Way of Seeing* by Margaret Mead and Rhoda
Metraux.

Stafford likes "this generous and energetic book" but
believes that the authors' views are "on the whole,
impractical to the point of naivete." She does not,
for example, share their optimistic faith in the
emergence of a new ethic that will bestow coherence on
the universal mind, nor does she believe in the
possibility of the adoption of a world-wide second
language, though she would like to, nor does she
believe that lowering the age of franchise to
eighteen, giving economic independence to all
students, and draft reform will erase the generation
gap.

D63   *Vogue*, 155 (June 1970), 72.

Rev. of *The Bay of Noon* by Shirley Hazzard.

She "has such a treasury of style that she can
economize or splurge, and, because her taste is
unerring, every expenditure is right."

D64   *Vogue*, 156 (15 Aug. 1970), 34.

Rev. of *A Certain World: A Commonplace Book* by W.H.
Auden.

This compendium of poetry and prose on subjects which
interested Auden throughout his life "is not to be
consumed all at once; it is to be quietly grazed for a
diversity of taste sensations—sweet, pungent, salt,
bittersweet. There is very little vinegar."

D65   "A Little Girl in a World Apart." *Book World*,
Washington (D.C.) *Post*, 23 Aug. 1970, p. 4.

Rev. of *Words for a Deaf Daughter* by Paul West.

"Paul West, who seems to have read everything, and considered everything (birds, mathematics, genetics, music, odd parts of the world and airplanes), uses the language with a combined ingenuity and precision, perfectly suiting his sentences and the words within them to the cadences of his moods as they are dictated by [his daughter's]: elegantly colloquial in their collaboration, father and daughter can rapidly cascade, can surge and recede like tides, lie still like a limpid lake."

D66   "Gooney Bird." *New York Review of Books*, 15 (8 Oct. 1970), 14-17.'

Rev. of *The Wartime Journals* of Charles A. Lindbergh.

Stafford objects to Lindberg's chronomania, vagueness, sententiousness, and his use of "comic strip American clichés." She concludes: "He is as American as cherry pie or the atomic bomb, courageous, suspicious, xenophobic ... wedded with great generosity of spirit to the conservation of animals and landscape, restless, inquisitive. But as an intransigent midwestern American, he is given to stereotypical and inattentive judgments...."

D67   *Vogue*, 156 (15 Oct. 1970), 34.

Rev. of *Frederick the Great* by Nancy Mitford.

In this book, Mitford "has refurbished the always fantastic and always fascinating story of Frederick the Great of Prussia with her particular idiom of sangfroid and wit and discreet erudition...."

D68   *Vogue*, 156 (1 Nov. 1970), 98.

Rev. of *Autobiography* by Enid Bagnold.

"Privileged and beautiful ... and loved, she is to be envied her flashing, jocular candour about herself and everyone she ever knew."

D69   "Birdbath." *New York Review of Books*, 15 (3 Dec. 1970), 26-27.

Rev. of *A White House Diary* by Lady Bird Johnson.

"The importance of her book is questionable; the political troubles that made the history of the Johnson years are handled without particularity; she is inept at the delineation of personality; she is too kind and too cautious to gossip; she responds with delight to anecdotes told her by others but she cannot compose any of her own. It is a harmless book, but it is very long."

Rev. of *A Woman of Quality: Eleanor Roosevelt* by Stella K. Hershan.

This book is "earnest and unoriginal and probably the writing of it gave the author pleasure."

D70   "Christmas Books for Children." *New Yorker,* 46 (5 Dec. 1970), 200, 203-06, 208-10, 213-20.

Stafford reviews the annual round up of children's books. Dorothea Straus (Hll) records one of Stafford's comments about these books: "Gosh darned sanitized pap! Give me the bad witches and demons, the scalding cauldrons and evil spells of the old days!"

1971

D71   *Vogue,* 158 (1 Sept. 1971), 282-83.

Rev. of *Thresholds* by Dorothea Straus.

"Her book is as shapely as an egg fashioned by Fabergé, enameled and begirt with jewels and filigree of gold, and fitted cleverly with hinges so that it may be opened to reveal a collection of miniatures: memories in the shape of lilies, grief, exuberance, uncertainty, amour propre in the shape of trees or roods or nightingales or coronets. But the lapidarian ornaments only enhance, they do not conceal the poise of the simplest form in nature. The writing itself, that is to say, is not ornamental, but the general effect is that of a picture gallery, hung richly if often quixotically--Brueghel side by side with Dürer, Vermeer next to Rubens."

D72   "Sensuous   Women."   *New   York Review of Books*, 17 (23
      Sept. 1971), 33-35.

      Rev. of *Kate Chopin, a Critical Biography* by Per
      Seyersted and *The Complete Works of Kate Chopin*, ed.
      Per Seyersted.

      Stafford agrees that Chopin "is deserving of a great
      deal more attention than she has received, partly
      because she was long before her time in dealing with
      sexual passion and the intricate familial and personal
      emotions of women, and partly because she is an
      uncommonly entertaining writer." (Stafford rebukes
      Seyerested for misusing the word "hopefully.")

D73   *Vogue*, 158 (Dec. 1971), 68.

      Rev. of *Eleanor and Franklin* by Joseph P. Lash.

      "The Hyde-Park Franklin and his cousin Eleanor Oyster-
      Bay Roosevelt were as unlike as a pea and a pecan that
      had   found   themselves,   through   some   freakish
      permutation, in the same pod or the same shell."

D74   "Children's   Books   for Christmas."   *New Yorker*, 47 (4
      Dec. 1971), 177-84, 187-88, 190, 193-94, 196, 199-200,
      202-04, 206, 209, 212, 214.

      See D70.

                              1972

D75   "Love Match of Pleasures: Eating and Reading."   *Vogue*,
      159 (1 Jan. 1972), 122.

      Rev. of *Among Friends* by M.K.F. Fisher.

      These memoirs reminded Stafford of her own childhood,
      but "There was one great difference: she was happy and
      fearless and I was unhappy and afraid."   Stafford
      speculates that the cause of this difference was that
      Fisher liked to eat (especially fried egg sandwiches),
      whereas the only food Stafford liked as a child was
      heavily salted raw potatoes.   Stafford concludes: "I
      envy Mrs. Fisher because she lives so well, and I envy
      her because she writes so well.   Right now I am
      famished, and I am going downstairs and make a fried

egg sandwich and have some raw potatoes on the side. Maybe then, with some honest grub sticking to my ribs, I can become a passable writer."

D76 "Is Old Age Wasted on the Old?" *Vogue*, 160 (July 1972), 108-09.

Rev. of *The Coming of Age* by Simone de Beauvoir.

Stafford finds this book to contain no new material on the problems of old age or suggestions for their amelioration. "The result is that her polemic seems to be addressed to someone or something (Someone up there whose name begins with 'G'?) to *blame* for the final season of existence. She looks upon it not as a condition but as an insult and an injury perpetrated by some big clowning roughneck, and it makes her cross as a bear." Nevertheless, Stafford agrees "wholeheartedly that the coming of age is, quite literally, a pain in the neck and it isn't fair and it is all God's fault for being such a wet blanket."

D77 "Living It Out." *New York Review of Books*, 19 (10 Aug. 1972), 22-26.

Rev. of *Piaf* by Simone Berteaut; *Coco Chanel: Her Life, Her Secrets* by Marcel Haedrich, tr. Charles L. Markmann; and *Paris Was Yesterday* by Janet Flanner.

"It is a refreshment to turn the eyes away from the febrile raptures and doldrums of Edith Piaf and the severity and joyless narcissism of Coco Chanel and to rest it on Janet Flanner's civilized appraisal of many lives lived in France, most of them by French and most of them by Parisians."

D78 "Enriching the Idiom." *Book World*, Washington (D.C.) *Post*, 17 September 1972, pp. 8, 10.

Rev. of *Black English: Its History and Usage in the United States* by J.L. Dillard.

"There is so much arresting and important information in *Black English* that the author's excessive use of turgid sociological lingo is a vexation and a hindrance to the reader.... Almost as distracting-- but considerably more entertaining--are Dillard's scholarly conniption fits over errors and racist insults perpetrated by his colleagues, dead and alive, but unfortunately in the midst of one of these expostulations, he commits the fashionable sin of misusing the word 'hopefully'.... To be sure, he at no time makes a plea for precision or for elegance of diction among those of any race, creed or color. Still a linguist . . ."

D79 "Christmas Books for Children." *New Yorker*, 48 (2 Dec. 1972), 190-92, 195-96, 198, 200, 202, 205-06, 208-12.

See D70.

D80 *Book World*, Washington (D.C.) *Post*, 17 Dec. 1972, pp. 1, 4.

Rev. of *Tallulah* by Brendan Gill.

Stafford recounts the major events in the life of Tallulah Bankhead, as given in Brendan Gill's "cool-headed and sympathetic" biography. She concludes by saying that "It must have been exhausting, exasperating, sometimes amusing, often repelling, heartbreaking to know her. But to read Brendan Gill on her is a wholly engrossing experience: fascinated by his subject, he fascinates his reader.... The book is more than a biography; it is a history of the good deeds and the shenanigans through which theatrical Tallulah raced at top speed until, literally out of breath, she died at the age of 66 of emphysema."

1973

D81 "Harry Truman Only His Family Knew." *Vogue*, 161 (Feb. 1973), 166.

Rev. of *Harry S. Truman* by Margaret Truman.

"While the presentation of its facts may not please the historians and will enrage the Republicans who won't read it but will complain about the price anyhow," Stafford, herself, finds it "a joy to read about a happy family. A family with no mush."

D82   "Anne Morrow Lindbergh's Ordeal."   *McCall's*, 100
       (March 1973), 80-81, 108-14.

       Rev. of *Hour of Gold, Hour of Lead* by Anne Morrow
       Lindberg.

       Stafford recounts the events which passed between
       March 1, 1932, when the infant Lindbergh was
       kidnapped, through April 3, 1936, when his murderer
       was executed.

D83   "No Place like Home." *Book World*, Washington (D.C.)
       Post, 1 April 1973, pp. 3, 10.

       Rev. of *We Have All Gone Away* by Curtis Harnack, *Ranch
       on the Laramie* by Ted Olson, *Hide and Seek* by Jessamyn
       West, and *Seven Houses: A Memoir of Time and Places* by
       Josephine W. Johnson.

       "These four books are four laments for the ravishment
       of the land, but they are not diatribes; they are
       pledges of thanksgiving that their authors weren't
       born yesterday."

       Stafford prefaces her remarks on West's book by
       mentioning that she spent three months with her in a
       trailer parked on the banks of the Colorado River near
       Mesquite, Texas.   Stafford did not share West's
       admiration of Thoreau: "...the deification of nature
       embarrasses me, and while Miss West is anything but
       maudlin, I find myself staring at my feet instead of
       at the royal sunset she is looking at.   And then,
       there is my discomfort in having that great big New
       England ghost around, putting in his two cents' worth
       every other page."

D84   *Book World*, Washington (D.C.) *Post*, 26 August 1973,
       pp. 1-3.

       Rev. of *A Lost Lady* by Willa Cather.

       Stafford prefaces this long review with a defense of
       the Middle West and with a biography of Cather.   She
       then gives a plot summary of the novel; she concludes:
       "In the 50 years since Willa Cather created him, Niel
       Herbert's [the protagonist's] dark vision of the
       desecration of the land has been realized odiously, so

much more odiously than he could possibly have imagined that we hope he did not live long enough to go back to his trammeled native ground. In 1923, readers of his sorrowful interior monologue would sorrow, but their experience would be literary and easily ameliorated. In 1973, while the reader is rapt with suspense and with admiration for the writer's deft spinning of her tale, afterward he mourns, and for a long time he hears *Dies irea, dies illa* being chanted by the winds in the cities of the plains where once stood trees."

D85 "Norman Mailer's Marilyn Monroe." *Vogue*, 162 (Sept. 1973), 288-89, 342-45.

Rev. of *Marilyn* by Norman Mailer.

After giving a very sympathetic portrait of Marilyn ("she would have brought out the mother in a stone"), whom she met one July afternoon in the 1950's at the house of Joseph Thorndike in Westport, Connecticut, Stafford says that "Mr. Mailer and his publishers should receive a hundred lashes from a bullwhip and then be pilloried for life for this ghoulish disinterment of a wretched, luckless creature."

D86 "Christmas Books for Children." *New Yorker*, 49 (3 Dec. 1973), 194, 197-200, 203-08, 210, 213-16, 218-20.

See D70.

1974

D87 "Anne Lindbergh: A Puzzlement." *Vogue*, 163 (March 1974), 38.

Rev. of *Locked Rooms and Open Doors* by Anne Lindberg.

This third volume of Lindberg's diaries and letters perplexes Stafford, who finds Lindbergh incomprehensibly uncertain of herself, in spite of her twenty-nine years of spectacular experience. She finds her "a superficial reporter of herself," and to Lindbergh's assertion that she cannot afford to be imaginative, that she has to live in a watertight compartment, Stafford queries, "If the only way to live is in watertight compartments, how are we to know when we have died?"

D88   "How the West Was Lost." *Book World*, Washington
       (D.C.) *Post*, 1 Sept. 1974, pp. 1-2.

       Rev. of *Centennial* by James A. Michener.

       Stafford criticizes the pretentiousness and long-
       windedness of this book: *"Ars longa, vita brevis
       est.* In the case of *Centennial*, the opposite
       obtains."

D89   "Children's Books for Christmas." *New Yorker*, 50 (2
       Dec. 1974), 170, 172, 175-76, 178, 182, 184, 187-88,
       190-94, 197-201, 203-04.

       See D70.

                            1975

D90   "Lives of Great Ones: Judy, Barbra, Bogie, and So
       Forth." *Esquire*, 84 (Oct. 1975), 90, 94, 96.

       Rev. of *Judy* by Gerald Frank.

       This book "brings on so many attacks of narcolepsy
       that it takes a very long time to get through."

       Rev. of *I'm the Greatest Star* by Rene Jordan.

       "A rugged individualist, a hell-bent-for-election
       iconoclast, Barbra Streisand dropped one of the a's of
       her given name to be different. This seems to be
       about the extent of her originality."

       Rev. of *Humphrey Bogart* by Nathaniel Benchley.

       Stafford does not like this book: "It is not so much
       that his portrait is poorly executed as it is that his
       sitter is such an oaf...."

       Rev. of *Bring on the Empty Horses* by David Niven.

       This book "is not all bad but there is far too much
       rice pudding for the raisins."

       Rev. of *Hollywood Babylon* by Kenneth Anger.

       This is "probably one of the dreariest dirty books I
       have ever read."

After reading so many books on Hollywood and its stars, Stafford doubts she "will ever voluntarily read another book on the subject--unless Marshall McLuhan should write a critical study of *King Kong* or Norman Mailer a biography of Marie Dressler."

D91 "Brownmiller on Rape: A Scare Worse Than Death." *Esquire*, 84 (Nov. 1975), 50, 52.

Rev. of *Against Our Will* by Susan Brownmiller.

"The want of mercy is a serious drawback in personality; so are tunnel vision (some other mighty fearful things are going on besides rape--famine, for example) and shrillness of voice. It is not to a writer's advantage to make categorical statements without buttressing them with proved examples, nor is it attractive to use arcane jargon without explaining it--the author under discussion speaks often of a cryptoscience heretofore unknown to me called 'victimology,' and she says that the sisterhood has 'politicized' rape. Perhaps Miss Brownmiller is a charmer, a wit, an engaging and scholarly raconteur, a looker, a clotheshorse, a good do-gooder. But she is not a lady and she is a very bad writer."

D92 "The Easy-to-Wrap, Relatively Cheap, Unbreakable Christmas Present." *Esquire*, 84 (Dec. 1975), 30, 33, 59-60.

Although Stafford calls herself a "Clausophobe" and yearns for the "abolition of Christmas," she has resigned herself to the annual return of "this unholy day of obligation." She has, to some extent, mitigated its complications by vowing that "This year, and in all years to come, everyone on my lists is going to get booze or books--I have scratched babies and illiterate teetotalers." She then lists several books which she deems suitable as Christmas presents, ranging from cookbooks and gardening books to dictionaries and works of fiction.

D93 "Children's Books for Christmas." *New Yorker*, 51 (1 Dec. 1975), 162, 166-68, 171-74, 176-78, 181-82, 184-88.

See D70.

1976

D94   "Scenes from a Great American Marriage." *Esquire*, 85
       (Jan. 1976), 19, 22.

       Rev. of *The Book of Abigail and John: Selected Letters
       of the Adams Family, 1762-1784.*

       "This chronicle is in every way remarkable--the story
       not only of individual survival during war" but also
       "of the triumphant survival of a marriage.... this
       husband and wife in their letters may have written the
       most powerful love story I have ever read...."

D95   "Playing Purr Gulf in the Third Reich." *Esquire*, 85
       (Feb. 1976), 12, 14.

       Rev. of *Golfing for Cats* by Alan Coren.

       In spite of Coren's beginning the second paragraph of
       his foreword with "Hopefully, *Golfing for Cats* ..." (a
       solecism which causes "a rabid reaction" in Stafford,
       even though she knows "all but seventy-nine persons in
       the English-speaking world now doggedly misuse the
       word"), Stafford continued to read the book and found
       British Coren "one of the funniest writers I have ever
       read from any country."

D96   "Tales of the Sixties Kid." *Esquire*, 85 (March 1976),
       28, 32.

       Rev. of *Kinflicks* by Lisa Alther.

       If Alther "had cut her report by a third (at least),
       had curbed her gluttony for irrationally farfetched
       scatological metaphor, discordant cornball wise-
       cracking; if she had hidden the tools with which she
       fashioned her symbols; if she had soft-pedaled her
       exuberant desire to share abstruse scientific fact and
       philosophic hypothesis--if, that is, she had been more
       courteous to her reader, *Kinflicks* might have been a
       work of considerable and even important substance
       instead of, as it is, an entertainment, half bulk and
       half froth."

       Rev. of *How to Get Balled in Berkeley* by Anne
       Steinhardt.

"Twenty times funnier than *Kinflicks*, it is twenty
times more serious."

D97   "The Pros of Cons." *Esquire*, 85 (April 1976), 24, 28.

Rev. of *Hustlers and Con Men* by Jay Robert Nash.

Although Stafford would not recommend buying this
book, she would recommend having a look at it "if it
happens to be on a coffee table in a house where you
are bored at a party. The subject [the confidence man
and his game] is universally and timelessly en-
thralling, since everybody is a potential, if not a
real, victim, and almost everybody is, as well,
potentially if not really fraudulent."

D98   "Richard Condon Scores Again." *Esquire*, 85 (May
      1976), 14, 20-21.

Rev. of *The Whisper of the Axe* by Richard Condon.

Stafford gives mostly a plot summary of this "peach of
an entertainment."

D99   "The Ballerina Who Loves Baked Beans." *Esquire*, 85
      (June 1976), 33.

Rev. of *Margot Fonteyn: An Autobiography*.

This book "is a testament to unswerving dedication to
an art, a humble but severely intransigent lifetime
pledge to a cult almost divinely sacred." Stafford
chuckles approvingly over Fonteyn's list of favorite
foods: "bread and butter, potatoes, cheese and baked
beans." Stafford says, "There is a piquant and
paradoxical chic in the thought of the Sleeping Beauty
breaking that long fast not with a collation of larks'
tongues but with a can of Heinz baked beans and a
chunk of rat cheese."

D100 "The Lardner Family: Were They Lost, Daddy?" *Esquire*,
      86 (July 1976), 14, 18-19.

Rev. of *My Family Remembered* by Ring Lardner, Jr.

Stafford gives a mainly descriptive account of this
book, which she praises as a "laconic and courtly

memoir presented ... without superlative or blame or praise."

D101   "Bertie in a Gilded Cage."   *Book World*, Washington (D.C.) *Post*, 25 July 1976, 1.

Rev. of *The Royal Victorians: King Edward VII, His Family and Friends* by Christopher Hibbert.

In "his marvelous new book" about "Queen Victoria's firstborn and namesake," who "was a tribulation to her from his nursery," Christopher Hibbert "clearly demonstrates why things could not have been otherwise. He accomplishes this without resorting to psychoanalytic theorizing, digressing briefly on such matters as Victorian boudoir furniture and the fare at picnics with such wry relish and horror that one wishes he would stray farther and longer."

D102   "Hammock Reading."   *Esquire*, 86 (Aug. 1976), 14, 16, 48.

Stafford begins this review with a reminiscence about her experience in grammar school, when one could win a letter to sew on a jacket by making one of the best reports on ten books read over the summer vacation.

Rev. of *Smart Aleck* by Howard Teichmann.

This is "an agreeable biography of Alexander Woollcott."

Rev. of *Nancy Mitford: A Memoir* by Harold Acton.

This book left Stafford feeling "shortchanged."

Rev. of *I Hear America Swinging* by Peter De Vries.

"He makes me sick with the god-awful truth he tells and sick with laughter...."

Rev. of *The People's Almanac* by David Wallechinsky and Irving Wallace.

"If your cortex really is aestivating, this omnium-gatherum will keep your happy for days, but it's chunky and awkward and would be hell in a hammock."

D103 "The Scarlett Letters." *Book World*, Washington (D.C.)
Post, 3 Oct. 1976, 1-2.

Rev. of *Margaret Mitchell's Gone With the Wind
Letters, 1936-1949*, ed. Richard Harwell.

"Open as she is, Miss Mitchell reveals herself hardly
at all in these letters. She says not a blessed thing
about what she did with all those millions she must
have made. It seems never to have occurred to her to
write another book, or a story, an essay, or a poem,
or a play. And the one book she did write was a
fluke--she'd read everything in the library except the
exact sciences so her husband brought her reams of
blank paper and told her to get to work."

D104 "Mrs. Hemingway Remembers." *Esquire*, 86 (Oct. 1976),
28, 30.

Rev. of *How It Was* by Mary Welsh.

Stafford does not like this autobiography by the
fourth wife of Ernest Hemingway, finding it "Immodest,
cliché-ridden, clogged with great chunks of
indigestible facts about boats, engines, guns and the
habits of wild animals." In the last line of the
book, Welsh speaks of her "lovely, satisfying work."
Stafford says, "It's that last line that gets my
dander up. People who, without proof of performance,
deify 'work' (the people I mean here are the ones who
declare themaelves as 'Writer' in their passports)
make me want to chew tobacco." Stafford concludes
with "Despite what foregoes, I do not like knocking
books. I know too well the labor that has gone into
the writing even when the finished product is lousy.
However, when a book deserves chastisement, when a
book that should have been revelatory, instructive,
that should, indeed, have been important, is silly, I
will give it no quarter." This book "is almost
exclusively awful."

Stafford says that this is the last review she will
write for *Esquire* and maybe the last she will ever
write (as it proved to be).

SECTION E

MISCELLANEA

This section lists some miscellaneous items, including (1) letters, (2) statements, (3) author's notes, (4) recordings, and (5) addresses.

1. LETTERS

E1 Letters to Robert Lowell. The Houghton Library, Harvard University, Cambridge, Mass.

Forty-seven letters from Jean Stafford to Robert Lowell, following their separation in August, 1946. C. David Heymann (H20) and Ian Hamilton (H19) paraphrase and quote from many of these letters.

E2 "Some Letters to Peter and Eleanor Taylor." *Shenandoah*, 30 (Autumn 1979), 27-55.

Twelve letters from June, 1940, to September 28, 1944, from Baton Rouge, La., New York City, Monteagle, Tenn., Yaddo, and Damariscotta Mills, Maine.

2. STATEMENTS

E3 "What's Wrong with the American Novel?" *American Scholar*, 24 (Autumn 1955), 464-503.

"This is the stenographic record of a discussion held at a private residence in Manhattan on Tuesday evening, July 26, 1955. Present were the following persons: Stephen Becker, Simon Michael Bessie, Ralph Ellison, Albert Erskine, Hiram Haydn, Jean Stafford, William Styron." (In truth, Stafford speaks very little.)

E4 "Topics: Women as Chattels, Men as Chumps." Editorial. New York *Times*, 9 May 1970, p. 24.

In this comment on "Fem Lib," Stafford agrees with the feminists on the necessity of equal pay for equal work,

of legal abortion, and of the establishment of day-care
centers. However, if "women have been treated as
chattels ... men have been treated as chumps." She
mentions alimony as one example. Men and women are
different, she goes on to say, and "gender is neither
an advantage nor an affliction but ... a fact."

E5   "Response." In "Symposium on the Teaching of Creative
      Writing--II." *Four Quarters,* 10 (Jan. 1961), 16.

Stafford expresses her opinion that creative writing
cannot be taught. However, she feels it may be valu-
able for the younger writer to have contact with
established writers. She considers that she, herself,
profited from listening to Ford Madox Ford, Robert
Frost, Sherwood Anderson, John Peale Bishop, and
others, when she worked as secretary to the writers'
conferences during several summers at the University of
Colorado.

E6   "A Statement." *Saturday Review,* 45 (6 Oct. 1962), 50.

Stafford responds to the newspaper story that, at the
encouragement of her husband A.J. Liebling, she had
"convinced" the other judges, Mr. Gannett and Mr. Gold,
to give Walker Percy's *The Moviegoer* the 1962 National
Book Award for fiction: "I wish to correct the impression that my husband bossed me in the first place
and I bossed Mr. Gannett and Mr. Gold in the second.
The jury reached a unanimous decision to grant the
award to Mr. Percy, whose novel all of us admire."

3.   AUTHOR'S NOTES

E7   Autobiographical note. In *New Short Novels.* Ed. Mary
      Louise Aswell. New York: Ballantine, 1954, p. 181.

E8   "Author's Note." *Bad Characters.* New York: Farrar,
      Straus and Giroux, 1964, pp. vii-viii.

Stafford does "not look on all the characters in these
stories as bad; some of them do have wicked hearts, but
as many of them are victims." Here Stafford also

acknowledges kinship with the protagonist of the title story: she is "someone I knew well as a child; indeed, I often occupied her skin...."

E9   "Author's Note." *The Mountain Lion*. New York: Farrar, Straus and Giroux, 1972, pp. xvii-xix.

Stafford says that when she finished *The Mountain Lion*, she felt deep remorse for what she had done to her heroine, Molly Fawcett. "Poor old Molly! I loved her dearly and I hope she rests in peace."

E10 "Author's Note." *The Collected Stories*. New York: Farrar, Straus and Giroux, 1969, pp. xi-xii.

After an autobiographical reminiscence, Stafford says: "Most of the people in these stories are away from home, too, and while they are probably homesick, they won't go back. In a sense, then, the geographical grouping I have chosen for the stories is arbitrary. I have borrowed titles from Mark Twain and Henry James ... who are two of my favorite American writers and to whose dislocation and whose sense of place I feel allied."

E11 "Note." In *Fat*. Coll. by Kit Reed. Indianapolis: Bobbs Merrill, 1974, pp. 60-61.

After her "The Echo and the Nemesis," Stafford affixes this note in which she explains that she knew little about obesity as a symptom of neurosis when she wrote this story: "To the writer of fiction, a little of Freud's hypotheses and those of his successors isn't seriously dangerous. More, however, is; and much is disastrous."

4.   RECORDINGS

E12 "Jean Stafford Reads One of Her Short Stories." New York: J. Norton Publishers (5-11716, RSS reel).

"Life Is No Abyss," recorded Y.M.-Y.W.H.A. Poetry Center, New York, in 1967.

5.   ADDRESSES

E13   "A Writer's Lament to Graduates: 'What I Would Give to
       Square a Root!'"   New York *Times*, 3 June 1979, p. 18.

       Excerpts from a commencement address delivered at
       Southampton College in 1973, as reported by the *East
       Hampton Star*. Stafford laments the deficiencies of her
       own education, especially the fact that she has read
       little science and has had little physical training.
       However, in her proposal for the ideal education, she
       says that the study of language is the most important:
       "Because it is upon the knowledge of language that
       knowledge itself depends. And the proper teaching of
       language   should   be   of   prime   concern   from   the
       kindergarten through the graduate school."

Part II
Works about Jean Stafford

SECTION F

CRITICISM

This section is divided into four parts: (1) general
criticism, (2) criticism of individual works, (3) foreign
criticism, and (4) dissertations. The first part lists all
works which deal with two or more of Stafford's works, or
which are concerned with some aspect of her work in general. The second part lists, first, the articles that have
been solely concerned with Stafford's books, and second,
analyses of her stories. All works are listed in alphabetical order, with the exception of the first part of
subsection 2, where Stafford's books are listed in chronological order.

1. GENERAL CRITICISM

F1 Aldridge, John W. *After the Lost Generation: A Critical Study of the Writers of Two Wars.* New York: McGraw-Hill, 1951. Pp. 195-97.

Stafford's *ML* is an illustration of the new novelists' turn away from the world of social manners in order to create "a separate and private moral context for each of their books and to find a meaning for the moral dilemma of their characters within that context."

F2 ————. *In Search of Heresy: American Literature in an Age of Conformity.* New York: McGraw Hill, 1956. Pp. 16, 22, 120.

Mentions Stafford as one of the writers of the postwar literary revival who wrote "their first books in a spirit of confidence that they were entering on a new creative cycle and carrying forward an established creative tradition" but who "suddenly found themselves high and dry in a world where all they stood for seemed to have gone into eclipse and where they themselves had become premature anachronisms."

F3 "The Art of the Short Story: Principles and Practices in the United States." In *American Writing Today: Its Independence and Vigor.* Ed. Allan Angoff. Freeport, New York: Books for Libraries, 1957. P. 184.

The author of this unsigned article from the *Times Literary Supplement* mentions Stafford as one of the good contemporary American short story writers who are little known in England at this time.

F4 Auchincloss, Louis. "Jean Stafford." In his *Pioneers and Caretakers: A Study of Nine American Women Novelists.* Minneapolis: University of Minnesota Press, 1965. Pp. 152-60.

81

Gives details of Stafford's biography and comments on her fiction. In discussing *BA*, he concentrates on its Proustian resemblances; he sees *ML* as her masterpiece, with its Molly being "one of the memorable children of American fiction"; the characters of *CW* seem to be "survivors from tales of Sarah Orne Jewett." He also comments on a few of the short stories, which he considers "beautiful pieces, almost without exception," yet he does not value them so highly as the novels. Stafford is "first and foremost a novelist."

F5   Bessie, Simon Michael. "America Writing Today: A Publisher's Viewpoint." *Virginia Quarterly Review*, 34 (Winter 1958), 1-17 [6].

Mentions Stafford as one of the younger novelists who have shown great promise.

F6   Cowley, Malcolm. "American Novels Since the War." In *The Arts at Mid-Century*. Ed. Robert Richman. New York: Horizon, 1954, pp. 243-250 [249].

Mentions Stafford as one of "the more talented" of the new fictionists; says that her *ML* has a theme typical of the new fiction: "the initiation of a pre-adolescent boy or girl into the knowledge of sex or evil."

F7   ————. "Critics Over Novelists." In his *The Literary Situation*. New York: Viking, 1954, pp. 59-73 [69].

Chastises Aldridge (F1) for not discussing Stafford and other novelists "who were already more important ... than most of those with whom he dealt at length."

F8   ————. "The 'New' Fiction: A Tidy Room in Bedlam." In his *The Literary Situation*. New York: Viking, 1954, pp. 43-58 [43, 47, 48]. Rpt. as "'Without any of the frayed edges.'" In *The Idea of an American Novel*. Ed. Louis D. Rubins and John Rees Moore. New York: Crowell, 1961, pp. 177-83 [179, 181].

Cites *ML* twice as an example of two characteristics of the new fiction: the use of an ingenue as central intelligence and the theme of the initiation of the pre-adolescent into the knowledge of sex or evil.

F9 Deegan, Dorothy Yost. *The Stereotype of the Single Woman in American Novels: A Social Study with Implications for the Education of Women.* New York: Octagon, 1969. P. 171.

Comments on Lucy Pride as a Boston spinster (*BA*).

F10 Eisinger, Chester E. *Fiction of the Forties.* Chicago: University of Chicago Press, 1963. Pp. 294-307.

Calling Stafford "the finest exemplar of the Jamesian tradition in her generation" (in her use of social satire, in her exploration of the maturation theme, and in her psychological and moral point of view), Eisinger points out that she was also influenced by Dostoevsky, Proust, and Austen. He sees the prevailing pattern in her fiction to be the conflict between two worlds: the clash of cultures in the outer world and the division of self in the inner world. He examines each of her three novels and *CABS*. He concludes by saying that Stafford's Jamesian manner made her "a writer of the new fiction, a writer for whom style always counts.... It is her style that is the enabling instrument in the fabrication of her irony and her symbols, that bares to us the truth of her psychological insights."

F11 Ellmann, Mary. *Thinking About Women.* New York: Harcourt Brace, 1968. Pp. 42, 134.

In her comments on "phallic criticism," Ellmann points out that while male critics consider sentiment a disadvantage, "the alternative of feminine coolness is found still more disagreeable.... Jean Stafford has sometimes been clinical...." Ellmann also discusses Stafford's *A Mother in History* as an example of how vehemently we react to the "unconscionable exploitation" of our stereotype of the Mother.

F12 French, Warren. "Introduction." In *20th-Century American Literature.* New York: St. Martin's, 1980, pp. 1-17 [10].

Mentions Stafford as one of the few new novelists of the generation of fictionists influenced by World War II who published their first works during the war.

F13   Fuller, Edmund. *Man in Modern Fiction: Some Minority Opinions on Contemporary American Writing*. New York: Random, 1958. P. 58.

Objects to Aldridge's assertion (F2), arguing that the "precise limitation of their various talents is that they never stood for anything."

F14   Hassan, Ihab H. "The Character of Post-War Fiction in America." *English Journal*, 51 (Jan. 1962), 1-8 [4]. Rpt. *Recent American Fiction: Some Critical Views*. Ed. Joseph J. Waldmier. Boston: Houghton Mifflin, 1963, Pp. 27-35 [31]. Rpt. *On Contemporary Literature*. Ed. Richard Kostelanetz. New York: Avon, 1964, Pp. 36-47 [41].

Lists ten types of the "rebel-victim," which he sees to be the central and controlling image of the contemporary novel, illustrating each type by reference to several novels which are "among the remarkable works of the last two decades." Gives *ML* as an example of the first type: "The hero as a child who may stand for truth or Edenic innocence, and is victimized ... by an ideal that society can never sanction or recognize"; gives *BA* as an example of the second type: "The lonely adolescent or youth, exposing the corrupt adult world...."

F15   _____. *Contemporary American Literature--1947-1972: An Introduction*. New York: Ungar, 1973. P. 64

Mentions Stafford as an example of a writer whose achievement is greater as a short story writer than as a novelist, commenting that her *CABS* provides an example of that achievement in "poignant decorum."

F16   _____. "The Idea of Adolescence in American Fiction." *American Quarterly*, 10 (Fall 1958), 312-24 [313, 324].

Lists Stafford's *BA* and *ML*, along with six other novels written after World War II in which "the image of adolescence throws a new light on that perennial conflict between the self and the world to which Freud assigned a decisive role in any culture." Sonia Marburg (*BA*) is a "promising example" of the present "effort to reinstate the American idea of adolescent initiation as a process leading to adult participation, leading to knowledge, sacrifice and responsibility."

F17   ————. "Jean Stafford: The Expense of Style and the Scope of Sensibility." *Western Review*, 19 (Spring 1955), 185-203.

Stafford's "incisive talent, her style so often distinguished" compel greater attention than she has received. She writes in the tradition of Proust and James most markedly, but the influence of Flaubert, Austen, and Dostoyevsky are also apparent. The center of her fiction is "a metaphor for age and childhood, a composite image of change and experience, caught in an ironic elegaic and retrospective vision. It is her attachment to this center that defines the expense of her style and the scope of her sensibility." Hassan discusses each of her three novels and the stories of *CABS* at some length; he appends a bibliography of Stafford's fiction up through 1953.

F18   ————. *Radical Innocence: Studies in the Contemporary American Novel*. Princeton: Princeton University Press, 1961. Pp. 70-72, 100.

Examines Stafford's three novels in terms of their treatment of childhood innocence, commenting most extensively on *ML*, even though he calls *BA* her "most impressive work." He defends the "excessive refinements of language," the "verbal dandyism" of Stafford, Capote, and Beuchner, suggesting that they are "a mode of invoking reality, not of evading it."

F19   Hills, Penney Chapin and L. Rust Hills, eds. *How We Live: Contemporary Life in Contemporary Fiction*. New York: Macmillan, 1968. P. 1004.

Includes Stafford's name in a list of some three hundred excellent writers of modern American fiction.

F20   Hoffman, Frederick J. *The Modern Novel in America, 1900-1950*. Chicago: Regnery, 1951. Pp. 27, 190.

Refers to Stafford as one example of the influence of Henry James's interest in form on modern fiction; *ML*, specifically, is evidence of Stafford's careful, though inferior, apprenticeship to Henry James and Edith Wharton.

F21   Janeway, Elizabeth.   "Women's Literature."   In *Harvard
       Guide to Contemporary American Writing*.   Ed. Daniel
       Hoffman.   Cambridge, Mass.: Harvard University Press,
       1979, pp. 342-395 [345, 352, 354].   Rpt. in her *Cross
       Sections from a Decade of Change*.   New York: Morrow,
       1982, pp. 187-242 [190, 197, 199].

       Janeway would "reckon Jean Stafford as an author of
       women's literature while noting with respect her
       rejection of the tenets of the women's liberation
       movement."   She includes Stafford as one of the
       "Distinguished women writers at work in the two decades
       of World War II [who] did much to express the matrix of
       feeling and judgment from which sprang the renewed
       self-consciousness of women which is typical of the
       later sixties and seventies."   In the work of none of
       these women writers is there any attempt to deal
       "consciously with feminist issues, but in their work
       can be found a steady, unromantic concentration on the
       immediate lived experience of women."   The situation of
       Stafford's women depends on their age: tomboys and
       "domineering old women who have lived past the years
       when they are expected to submit to the traditional
       role of Happy-Wife-and-Motherdom" enjoy their freedom,
       but "the area outside the conventional role is bleak."

F22   Jenson, Sid.   "The Noble Wicked West of Jean Stafford."
       Western American Literature, 7 (Winter 1973), 261-70.

       Places Stafford in "a long tradition of American
       writers who have ambivalent attitudes about East and
       West, about civilization and primitive nature.   Miss
       Stafford, like Cooper, Twain, and James, has visceral
       and cerebral attractions which simultaneously draw her
       to the city and to the country.   This tension creates
       in her fiction a dramatic depth typical of much good
       Western fiction."

F23   Kazin, Alfred.   *Bright Book of Life: American Novelists
       and Storytellers from Hemingway to Mailer*.   Boston:
       Little, Brown, 1973.   Pp. 174, 258n.

       The   "fiction   of   sensitiveness"   is   "usually
       distinguished by its too conscious style," which
       "offers an illusion of control." In Stafford's stories
       and in *BA*, her "style is a leading character."

F24   ————. *Contemporaries*.   Boston: Little,   Brown,
       1962. P. 210.

       Stafford is an example of those novelists of the
       forties whose books, under the influence of Henry
       James, reflected a "rage of style." Stafford "has of
       late years often seemed to bury herself in fine
       phrases."

F25   McCormick, John. *Catastrophe and Imagination*. London:
       Longmans, Green, 1955. P. 306.

       "In America the social challenge is often answered ...
       by watered-down versions of the Jamesian sensibility in
       a novel like Jean Stafford's *The Catherine Wheel*, and
       the allied work of the *New Yorker* ladies with elaborate
       memories of childhood, quaintly furnished houses, and
       delicately conveyed emotions--writing which merits the
       slander on James contained in the quip that he chewed
       more than he bit off."

F26   Magny, Claude-Edmonde. *The Age of the American Novel:*
       The Film Aesthetic of Fiction Between the Two Wars.
       Tr. by Eleanor Hochman.   New York: Ungar, 1972.   Pp.
       227-28.

       Passing mention of *BA*.

F27   Milne, Gordon. *The Sense of Society: A History of the*
       American Novel of Manners. Cranbury, N.J.: Associated
       University Presses, 1977. Pp. 254-55, 271n.

       Mentions *BA* and *CW* in his chapter on recent exemplars
       of the novel of manners: "...echoing Marquand in locale
       and character type, Miss Stafford echoes him as well in
       registering objections to the vulgar present, whose
       manners lack the individuality of taste of earlier
       times."

F28   Oates, Joyce Carol.   "The Interior Castle: The Art of
       Jean Stafford's Short Fiction." *Shenandoah*, 30 (Autumn
       1979), 61-64.

       "Subdued and analytical and beautifully-constructed,"
       Stafford's stories "are not to be too quickly grasped,
       too glibly assessed.   The 'interior castle' of
       Stafford's art is one which will repay close scrutiny

for its meanings open slowly outward, and each phrase,
each word, is deliberately chosen."

F29 Peden, William. *The American Short Story: Front Line
     in the National Defense of Literature*. Boston:
     Houghton Mifflin, 1964. Pp. 21, 30, 32, 89, 98-102,
     112, 187.

     "The smell of the sick room" permeates Stafford's *CABS*
     and *S*. "Her world is a limited one into which sunlight
     and fresh air seldom penetrate." Peden discusses
     Stafford in his chapter, "Sick in Mind and Body Both,"
     but says that she could have been placed as well in the
     chapter, "Jane Austens of Metropolis and Suburbia."

F30 ————. *The American Short Story, 1940-1975: Front
     Line in the National Defense of Literature*. Boston:
     Houghton Mifflin, 1975. Pp. 5, 12, 19, 21, 27, 70, 83-
     85, 97, 99, 186.

     Extends the comments of F29 to *BC* and *CS*.

F31 Ross, Danforth. *The American Short Story*. University
     of Minnesota Pamphlets on American Writers.
     Minneapolis: University of Minnesota Press, 1961. P.
     40.

     Mentions Stafford as one of the many contributors to
     the "sheer volume of good stories" that have been
     published in the Twentieth Century.

F32 Schwartz, Delmore.   "The Grapes of Crisis." In his
     Selected Essays.   Ed. Donald A. Dike and David H.
     Zucker. Chicago: University of Chicago Press, 1970,
     pp. 377-85 [380].

     One of the characteristics of modern literature is the
     appearance of a particular kind of heroine: in contrast
     with the beauty, innocence, and virtue of Henry James's
     heroines, "the truly glamorous modern heroine begins
     with cynicism and self-doubt as we can see in the
     fiction of Mary McCarthy, Carson McCullers, and Jean
     Stafford."

F33 ————. "Smile and Grin, Relax and Collapse."
     Selected Essays. Ed. Donald A. Dike and David H.
     Zucker. Chicago: University of Chicago Press, 1970.
     Pp. 412-17 [413].

Stafford is one of a group of writers who illustrate "the fact that when good writers write for *The New Yorker*, they adopt attitudes and mannerisms which are absent from their serious writing elsewhere. Most of these writers are striving in one guise or another--or none at all--to write their memoirs, although they are authors who in their writings elsewhere manage to distinguish very well between fiction and personal history...."

F34 Scott, Nathan A., Jr. "Black Literature." In *Harvard Guide to Contemporary American Writing.* Ed. Daniel Hoffman. Cambridge, Mass.: Harvard University Press, 1979, pp. 287-341 [295].

Mentions Stafford as one of the "many representative American writers" who responded to "the new vogue of Henry James," by "choosing to seek their effects by the unsaid and the withheld, by the dryly ironic analogy and the muted voice."

F35 ————. *Modern Literature and the Religious Frontier.* New York: Harper & Brothers, 1958. Pp. 94, 96, 97, 100.

Stafford is one of the writers of the last several years who want "to tell us that the particular quarry from which we are to derive the deepest insights into the meaning of human existence is the realm of dialogue, the realm of personal experience." These novelists do not write novels of society or politics but dwell "upon the relationships and the dilemmas of the private life, the psychological penalties exacted by loneliness and the need for love." This interest is reflected especially in their frequent use of the theme of childhood. Stafford shares with many of these novelists a "kind of richly personal complexity of style."

F36 Spiller, Robert E. et al., eds. *Literary History of the United States.* 4th ed., rev. New York: Macmillan, 1974. P. 1463.

BA is an example of the "new elegance" found in the novel of manners, which predominated in the late forties and early fifties. Responding to the "Jamesian precepts of style, structure, hidden implication," and cultivating "an elegance of sensibility," the novel of

manners at this time also "tended to become at once too
delicate and bizarre."

F37   Stevick, Philip. "Scheherazade Runs Out of Plots, Goes
       on Talking; the King Puzzled, Listens: An Essay on New
       Fiction." *Tri-Quarterly*, 26 (Winter 1973), 332-62 [340-
       49].

       In his attempt to define the "new fiction" of writers
       like Donald Barthelme, Richard Brautigan, and Robert
       Coover, Stevick analyzes the opening paragraph of
       Stafford's "A Country Love Story," which he sees to be
       "not only characteristic of her work as a whole. It
       also sounds like countless other stories of about the
       same period." Stafford's fiction is what the new
       fiction is not. He comments specifically on the fol-
       lowing characteristics of her fiction: its durational
       quality; its use of the "man-nature dichotomy, as a
       center for a symbolistic charge of meaning"; its fasci-
       nation "with the material objects of daily, sensory
       existence"; its "obsessive, house-bound quality"; its
       style; and its use of epiphanic form.

F38   Straumann, Heinrich. *American Literature in the
       Twentieth Century*. 3rd rev. ed. New York: Harper &
       Row, 1965. P. 126.

       CW exemplifies "psychosymbolical realism," a trend in
       fiction in the early fifties.

F39   Stuckey, William Joseph. *The Pulitzer Prize Novels: A
       Critical Backward Look*. Norman, Okla.: University of
       Oklahoma Press, 1981. Pp. 166, 230-33.

       The 1970 Pulitzer jury preferred *Them* by Joyce Carol
       Oates, but the Advisory Board cast its vote for
       Stafford's *CS*. Stafford's "preoccupation with the
       theme of illness--physical, mental, emotional--and with
       what might be called the snobbery of abberant behavior"
       provides a kind of unity to these stories.

F40   Vickery, Olga. "Jean Stafford and the Ironic Vision."
       South Atlantic Quarterly, 61 (Autumn 1962), 484-91.

       "Among contemporary writers Jean Stafford has merited
       considerable critical attention and received surpris-
       ingly little." Like Eudora Welty and Carson McCullers,

Stafford is "fascinated by the image of childhood and adolescence; by the misfit or freak who dramatizes isolation, loneliness, and inversion; and by the poignant quest of the individual for understanding and love." Stafford's difference, however, lies in her firm commitment "to the ironic vision of the external world of manners and the internal world of psychological process."

F41 ————. "The Novels of Jean Stafford." *Critique*, 5 (Spring-Summer 1962), 14-26.

"The novels of Jean Stafford have not received the detailed attention which they deserve." Vickery discusses each of Stafford's novels at length, showing how she uses her "protagonists--aliens, rebels, and freaks--as focal points in her exploration of the condition of the modern world."

F42 Vidal, Gore. "Ladders to Heaven: Novelists and Critics of the 1940's." In his *Rocking the Boat*. Boston: Little, Brown, 1962, pp. 125-46 [143].

Includes Stafford in his comments on "the distinguished second rank of younger writers" who have shown "much virtuosity and potentiality." Stafford, "though currently obsessed with literary interior decoration, has in such stories as 'The Echo and the Nemesis' displayed a talent which makes all the more irritating her recent catalogues of bric-a-brac, actual and symbolic."

F43 Voss, Arthur. "The Short Story since 1940: Eudora Welty, Mary McCarthy, Jean Stafford, J. F. Powers, J.D. Salinger, Bernard Malamud, and Flannery O'Connor." In his *The American Short Story: A Critical Survey*. Norman, Oklahoma: The University of Oklahoma Press, 1973, pp. 302-43 [312-14]; also see p. 284.

Stafford "combines an intellectuality somewhat similar to that of Mary McCarthy with a sensitivity and a style reminiscent of Katherine Ann Porter." The major theme of Stafford's stories is alienation and loss. If these stories "seem sometimes overly depressing, they have truth, and they are the work of a highly talented and disciplined artist."

F44   West,   Ray   B.,   Jr.   *The Short Story in America: 1900-
      1950.*   Chicago: Regnery, 1952.   P. 109.

      Lists   Stafford   along   with   several   other   young
      contemporary   writers   of   the   short   story,   who   are   in
      mid-career.

F45   Witham,   W.   Tasker.   *The   Adolescent   in the American
      Novel: 1920-1960.*   New York: Ungar, 1964.   Pp. 16, 61,
      68-69, 77-78, 98, 101, 189, 198-99, 204, 207, 225, 227,
      230, 240, 262, 265, 270, 271.

      Discusses   *BA*   and   *ML*   as   examples   in   many   of   his
      categories.

                 2.   CRITICISM OF INDIVIDUAL WORKS

Boston Adventure

F46   Mann, Jeanette W.   "Toward New Archetypal Forms: *Boston
      Adventure.*"   *Studies in the Novel,* 8 (Fall 1976), 291-
      303.

      Argues that Stafford has been neglected because she is
      "presenting a new kind of truth," and "that, as with
      the work of many women writers, new structures and a
      new   vocabulary   are   necessary   to   understand   it."
      Analyzes Sonia Marburg's journey toward consciousness
      in terms of Erich Neumann's *The Great Mother: An
      Analysis of the Archetype.*

The Mountain Lion

F47   Burns,   Stuart L.   "Counterpoint in Jean Stafford's *The
      Mountain Lion.*"   *Critique,* 9 (Spring 1967), 20-32.

      This is "not only a novel of adolescent initiation but
      a   saga   of   a   changing   America....   Through   a contra-
      puntal structure, Miss Stafford has depicted the disas-
      trous fate awaiting the uncompromising innocent in his
      encounter with modern society, while pointing out that
      a loss of innocence and a compromise of ideals go hand
      in hand."

F48 Gelfant,   Blanche H.   "Revolutionary   Turnings: *The
     Mountain   Lion   Reread*."   *Massachusetts   Review*,   20
     (Spring 1979), 117-25.

     Discusses the novel as social satire within the
     tradition of the American Western.   Considers *ML*
     revolutionary not only in its chosen literary tradition
     but also in its social consciousness: Stafford could
     imagine no other end for Molly but death; "Today we can
     imagine what thirty years ago Jean Stafford could not--
     a future for Molly.... The possibility of a life for
     Molly that we can now imagine into the novel gives it
     its most radical and hopeful turning upon itself, and
     revitalizes as it revolutionizes us as readers."

F49 Pilkington, William T.   "Introduction." *The Mountain
     Lion*. Albuquerque: University of New Mexico Press,
     1977, pp. vii-xv. Rpt. in his *Critical Essays on the
     Western American Novel*. Boston: G.K. Hall, 1980.   Pp.
     182-86.

     Analyzes this "authentic example of a rare but
     legendary kind of book: the neglected classic" for its
     ironic depiction of the West and as an initiation
     story.

The Catherine Wheel

F50 Mann, Jeanette W.   "Toward New Archetypal Forms: Jean
     Stafford's *The Catherine Wheel*."   *Critique*, 17 (Dec.
     1975), 77-92.

     Analyzes the narrative method, pattern of symbols, and
     theme of *CW*.   "Katharine Congreve represents a common
     type in Jean Stafford's fiction.   The heroines of her
     earlier novels and most of the major female characters
     in her short stories also deliberately turn their back
     on life.   Stafford has, as yet, presented only the
     conventional motivation for and consequences of the
     denial of the self; she has offered no alternatives."

A Winter's Tale

F51 Aswell, Mary Louise, ed. *New Short Novels*. New York:
     Ballantine, 1954. Pp. vi-vii.

     Aswell tells of the several revisions through which *WT*
     passed.   Comments that "Jean Stafford is in the direct

line of succession from Henry James, however individual
her style and content.... We feel that a significant
piece of literature would have been lost if this story
had remained unpublished."

Individual Short Stories

F52   Abrahams, William, ed. "Introduction." *Prize Stories,
      1980: The O. Henry Awards.* Garden City, New York:
      Doubleday, 1980, pp. 7-10 [9].

      Comments on "An Influx of Poets."

F53   Auchincloss, Louis. "Introduction." *Fables of Wit and
      Elegance.* New York: Scribner's, 1972, pp. vii-xii
      [xii].

      Comments on "The Echo and the Nemesis."

F54   Brickell, Herschel, ed. "Introduction." *Prize
      Stories, 1951: The O. Henry Awards.* Garden City, New
      York: Doubleday, 1951, pp. vii-xxvi [xv].

      Comments on "A Country Love Story."

F55   Cassill, R.V. *Instructor's Handbook: The Norton
      Anthology of Short Fiction.* New York: Norton, 1977.
      Pp. 188-91.

      Comments on "In the Zoo."

F56   Condon, Richard A. "Stafford's 'The Interior Castle.'"
      Explicator, 15 (Oct. 1956), 6.

      Examines the parallels between "The Interior Castle"
      and St. Theresa's *The Interior Castle.*

F57   Engle, Paul and Hansford Martin, eds. "Introduction."
      Prize Stories, 1955: The O. Henry Awards. Garden City,
      New York: Doubleday, 1955, pp. 9-12 [9].

      Comments on "In the Zoo."

F58   Fox, Hugh. "Standards: Some Subjectivities on
      Fiction." *Southern Humanities Review,* 7 (Spring 1973),
      183-90 [183-84].

Comments on "In the Zoo": In this story, "Jean Stafford is saying TYRANNY IS IN OUR MINDS. Which is a very important truth."

F59 Gettmann, Royal A. and Bruce Harkness. *Teacher's Manual for* A Book of Stories. New York: Rinehart, 1966. Pp. 59-60.

Comments on "A Reunion."

F60 Giroux, Robert. "A Note on 'Woden's Day.'" *Shenandoah*, 30 (Autumn 1979), 5.

"Woden's Day" and "An Influx of Poets" were extracted from Stafford's unfinished novel, *The Parliament of Women*.

F61 Gold, Herbert and David L. Stevenson, eds. *Stories of Modern America*. New York: St. Martin's Press, 1961. Pp. 337, 351.

Comments and study questions on "The Interior Castle."

F62 Hall, James B. and Joseph Langland, eds. *The Short Story*. New York: Macmillan, 1956. Pp. 357-59.

Comments on "Children Are Bored on Sunday."

F63 Hamalian, Linda and Leo Hamalian, eds. "Introduction." *Solo: Women on Women Alone*. New York: Delacorte, 1977, pp. 13-24 [19].

Comments on "I Love Someone."

F64 Havighurst, Walter. *Instructor's Manual for* Masters of the Modern Short Story. 2nd ed. New York: Harcourt, 1955, pp. 42-43.

Comments on "A Summer Day."

F65 Hollander, John. "Introduction." *American Short Stories Since 1945*. New York: Harper & Row, 1968, pp. ix-xviii [xiv].

Comments on "The Interior Castle."

F66   O'Faolain, Sean, ed.   *Short   Stories: A   Study   in*
      Pleasure. Boston: Little, Brown, 1961. Pp. 234-35.

      Gives six study questions on "A Country Love Story."

F67   Peden, William.   "Introduction."   *Stories* by   Jean
      Stafford,   John   Cheever,   Daniel   Fuchs,   and   William
      Maxwell.   New York: Farrar, Straus & Giroux, 1966, pp.
      v-viii [vii-viii].

      Comments on "Beatrice Trueblood's Story."   Peden says
      that he knows of no one who writes "with more insight
      than she of the limbo of the unloved, unwanted, and
      rejected individuals...."

F68   ————.   *Twenty-Nine   Stories*.   2nd   ed.   Boston:
      Houghton, 1967. Pp. 327-28.

      Comments and study questions on "A Country Love Story."

F69   Schulman, L.M.   "Preface."   *Autumn Light: Illuminations*
      of Age.   New York: Crowell, 1978, pp. ix-xi [x].

      Comments on "The Home Front."

F70   Sohn, David., ed.   "Introduction."   *Ten Modern American*
      Short Stories. New York: Bantam, 1965, pp. 1-10 [2-3].

      Comments on "The Scarlet Letter."

F71   Solomon, Barbara H.   "Introduction."   *The Experience of*
      the American Woman.   New York: New American Library,
      1978, pp. 1-29 [15].

      Comments on "Beatrice Trueblood's Story."

F72   Thorburn, David, ed.   *Initiation: Stories   and Short*
      Novels on Three Themes.   2nd ed.   New York: Harcourt,
      1976. Pp. 422-23.

      Study questions on "A Country Love Story."

3. FOREIGN CRITICISM

F73   Dommergues, Pierre.   *Les Écrivains américains*
d'aujourd'hui. Paris: Presses Universitaires de France,
1965. P. 37.

F74   Freese, Peter.   *Die amerikanische Kurzgeschichte nach*
1945: Salinger, Malamud, Baldwin, Purdy, Barth.
Frankfurt: Athaenäum Verlag, 1971. Pp. 31, 47.

F75   ————. *Die Initiationsreise: Studien zum jugendlichen*
Helden in Modernen amerikanischen Roman. Neümunster:
Karl Wachholtz Verlag, 1971. Pp. 61-62, 81-82, 86, 88,
169, 247, 271.

F76   Häusermann, Hans W.   "James Jones and Jean Stafford:
Rothaut   und   Bleichgesicht   in   der   amerikanischen
Tradition."   In his *Moderne amerikanische Literatur:*
Kritische Aufzeichnungen.   Francke Verlag Bern und
Munchen, 1965, pp. 95-97. See also pp. 64, 137, 143.

F77   Heller, Arno.   *Odyssee zum Selbst: Zur Gestaltung*
jugendlicher Identitätssuche im neuren amerikanischen
Roman.   Innsbruck: Inst. f. Sprachwissenschaft d.
Univ. Innsbruck, 1973. P. 168.

F78   Magny, Claude-Edmonde.   *L'Âge du roman américain*.
Paris: Editions du Seuil, 1948. P. 247.

F79   *Romanciers Américains contemporains*.   Paris: Didier,
1946. Pp. 277, 313.

F80   Saporta, Marc.   *Histore du roman américain*.   Nouvelle
ed. Paris: Gallimard, 1976. P. 499.

F81   Simon, Jean.   "Conclusion--Aujourd'hui."   In his *Le*
Roman américain au XXe siècle.   Paris: Boivin, 1950.
Pp. 181-84 [83].

4. DISSERTATIONS

F82   Avila, Wanda. "The Ironic Fiction of Jean Stafford."
      Ph.D., University of Maryland, 1980 [Abstract in
      Dissertation Abstracts International, 41 (November
      1980), 2108A].

F83   Burns, Stuart Leroy. "The Novel of Adolescence in
      America, 1940-1963."   Ph.D., The University of
      Wisconsin, 1964 [Abstract in *Dissertation Abstracts*,
      25 (October 1965), 2507A].

      Focuses on *ML*.

F84   Shinn, Thelma Jean Wardrop.   "A Study of Women
      Characters in Contemporary American Fiction, 1940-
      1970." Ph.D., Purdue, 1972 [Abstract in *Dissertation
      Abstracts International*, 34 (July 1973), 338].

      Comments on the major women characters in the fiction
      of several writers, including Stafford.

F85   White, Barbara Anne.   "Growing Up Female: Adolescent
      Girlhood in American Literature." Ph.D., University of
      Wisconsin-Madison, 1974 [Abstract in *Dissertation
      Abstracts International*, 35 (March 1975), 6167A].

      Focuses on *ML*.

SECTION G

REVIEWS OF BOOKS BY JEAN STAFFORD

This section lists reviews of Jean Stafford's books. They are listed by book reviewed (in chronological order of publication) and alphabetically within the listings for each title. If the review includes a portrait of Stafford, that fact is indicated at the end of the annotation.

1. BOSTON ADVENTURE

G1 "Better Than Its Boston." *Commonweal*, 40 (13 Oct. 1944), 615-16.

This is "a moving, serious and poetic novel." There are "a few discordant passages--a trivial word annoys at times, and more often a pompous word. But the discord is something excellent. Miss Stafford is not afraid of the grand manner, of the long sentence deliberately and calmly unfolding its clauses. The incidents of the first narrative are recalled, developed and explained in the meditative second half of the book. Again and again this scrutiny of the past, of the past acting on and determining the present, provides a very rich and sonorous material which is worked upon with deliberation and art.... In Miss Stafford's mind and style we are deeply interested."

G2 Blakeston, Oswell. *Life & Letters*, 51 (Dec. 1946), 200-02 [202].

"Well done for those who can read well."

G3 *Booklist*, 41 (1 Oct. 1944), 42.

The novel "has more than a tinge of morbidity and its sophistication is superficial. For readers with a taste for psychological characterization."

G4 Bullock, Elizabeth. "A New and Radiant Feminine Stylist." *Chicago Sun Book Week*, 24 Sept. 1944, p. 1.

Stafford is "an exceptional and original feminine talent." However, this book should be classified as a "fine psychological study, a triumph of stylistic virtuosity," but not as a novel because the plot lacks resolution.

G5   Cannon, Lee E. "Sentimental Journey." *Christian Century*, 61 (1 Nov. 1944), 1255-56.

The novel's satirical treatment of Boston society is "heavy and lacking in humor," and the novel is at times repetitious, with too much detail. Its virtues are its "penetrating and trenchant" characterization, and its "graceful, skillfully handled prose, full of charming phrasings and expressions."

G6   *Catholic World*, 160 (Dec. 1944), 283.

In "this outstanding first-novel of 1944," a "few spiritual props would not be out of place."

G7   *Commonweal*, 41 (20 Oct. 1944), 20.

This novel is "the most interesting novel of the season," being "most notable for its literary style."

G8   Curtiss, Mina. "Beacon Hill Brahmins." Boston *Globe*, 11 Oct. 1944, p. 17.

Although this is "an exceptionally clever first novel," Stafford's picture of Boston lacks signif-icance and authenticity; she adopts some externals of Proust's method without adopting its essence; and the book has a "humorless, almost hysterical quality."

G9   Feld, Rose. *New York Herald Tribune Weekly Book Review*, 24 Sept. 1944, p. 6.

The virtues of this novel are its intensity of feeling, sensitivity, perceptiveness, and magnetism; its defects are repetitiousness, wordiness, and lack of clear intent and resolution. Portrait.

G10 Fleischer, Lenore. *Publisher's Weekly*, 191 (30 Jan. 1967), 113.

This is a novel "of grace, wit, and poignant charm."

G11 Hackett, Alice. "New Novelists of 1944." *Saturday Review*, 28 (17 Feb. 1945), 12-14, 41 [13, 41].

Mainly a descriptive review of several American first novels of 1944. Portrait.

G12   Hackett, Francis. "Collision with Boston." New York
      Times, 23 Sept. 1944, p. 17, portrait. Rpt. in his *On
      Judging Books, in General and Particular.* Freeport,
      New York: Books for Libraries, 1974, pp. 234-36.

      "Not only is Jean Stafford determined to write
      literature at any cost, but she is also determined to
      give us tons of whipped cream on it."

G13   Jones, Howard Mumford. "The Artistry of Jean
      Stafford." *Saturday Review*, 27 (23 Sept. 1944), 10.

      Stafford is "a commanding talent, who writes in the
      great tradition of the English novel." *BA* has "the
      concentrated emotional power of the Brontës." Its
      style is "condensed, old-fashioned in its dignity,
      highly accurate as a report on the sensibilities of
      the 'I' who tells the story." Portrait.

G14   Kazin, Alfred. "Art and Resistance." *New Republic*,
      111 (23 Oct. 1944), 538, 540.

      This "remarkably fine novel" has "a distinction, as I
      see it, that springs from the meeting of genuine per-
      sonal culture with deep independence of sight." Like
      Proust's work, the novel is an epic of will in that
      through a higher cultivation and will Sonia transcends
      the destructive effects of childhood. Here, "at last,
      is a novel in which sensibility is not sacrificed to
      representation: in which the inwardness of man, at
      once the deposit of events and the shaper of them, is
      functionally related to bold and objective visual
      power." Although "Miss Stafford is not Proust, and
      her method has many suggestive limitations ... she is
      an extraordinarily talented novelist, and her book
      will give pleasure to sensitive readers."

G15   Kennedy, John S. "Fiction in Focus." *Sign*, 24 (Sept.
      1944), 112.

      "The first part of this unhackneyed book reminds one
      of *A Tree Grows in Brooklyn*, the second of the
      Marquand scapel jobs on Boston."

G16   *Kirkus Reviews*, 12 (15 July 1944), 302.

      "A futile sort of book, with an underlying bitterness
      of spirit."

G17   Maxwell, Joseph.   "Back   Bay Blues."   *America*, 71 (30
      Sept. 1944), 619.

      "The characters are well drawn, finely sustained, all,
      or practically all, are true to the tradition of an
      older, snobbish Boston."

G18   Miller, Aloysius J., S.J.   *Best   Sellers*, 4 (1 Nov.
      1944), 140.

      "Discriminating adults interested in what might have
      been going on behind the closed doors of Boston
      mansions before the rise of Hitler will enjoy the
      story."

G19   "Miss Pride's Companion."   *Newsweek*,   24 (25 Sept.
      1944), 102-03.

      Many of the usual faults of the first novel are here--
      wordiness, for example, but it is a "remarkable"
      novel, nevertheless, because "it is so richly imagi-
      native and   so   incisive in   its delineation of
      character" and because of its craftsmanship.   Brief
      biography and portrait.

G20   *New Yorker*, 20 (23 Sept. 1944), 78.

      The   many   parallels   between   *BA*   and   Proust   are
      "astonishing," even though this novel "stands cleanly
      and brilliantly on its own."   Stafford is "a writer of
      unmistakable endowment."

G21   Page,   Ruth.   "Some Proustian Images of Boston."   *New
      York Times Book Review*, 24 Sept. 1944, p. 3.

      Stafford, like Proust, is able to imbue detail with
      symbolic values.   The reader feels no emotional ident-
      ification with any of the characters: "They are ele-
      ments in a composition, seen at one remove, as in
      abstract painting the real objects which suggest the
      subject are, in the work itself, subservient to the
      subject."

G22   Prescott,   Orville.   "Outstanding   Novels."   *Yale
      Review*, n.s.34 (Autumn 1944), 189-92 [190].

The influence of both Dostoevsky and John P. Marquand is apparent in this "unsuccessful but ambitious first novel that reveals a considerable unorganized talent."

G23 "Proust on Pinckney Street." *Time*, 45 (22 Jan. 1945), 94, 96, 98.

The novel is Proustian in its sentence structure, philosophical overtones, and use of fantasy as a literary method. Its largest deficiency is its lack of plausibility. "Author Stafford is forever at a window sipping tea and day dreaming." Portrait.

G24 Spencer, Theodore. "Recent Fiction." *Sewanee Review*, 53 (Spring 1945), 297-304 [302-03].

Stafford in many ways merits her comparison with Proust, but the book does not deserve "all the praise it has received" because it is very "un-Proustian" in other ways. For example, it has something unreal about it (Chichester does not exist); it makes mistakes of detail (a Miss Pride would not live on Pinckney Street); and the characters become puppet-like.

G25 Taylor, Helene S. *Library Journal*, 69 (Aug. 1944), 651.

"Although the tale is tenuously extended, the characterizations are discerning and authentic."

G26 Trilling, Diana. "A New Talent." *Nation*, 159 (30 Sept. 1944), 383. Rpt. in her *Reviewing the Forties*. New York: Harcourt, 1978, pp. 107-09.

Stafford is "a remarkable new talent," but the novel as a whole is "strangely disappointing." The influence of Proust is most significantly reflected in the book's "dignity and flexibility of manner." The first half of the book is admirable because of its lack of autobiographical taint, or self-pity and sentimentality, but the second half is unsatisfactory because of its lack of objectivity and because introspection is substituted for action and conflict. Yet Stafford has "so much style and energy and intelligence" that she deserves "to be read and applauded."

G27   Wanning,   Andrews.   *Partisan   Review,* 11 (Fall 1944),
       474–77.

       Stafford, in this "unusual and absorbing first novel,"
       can be compared with Proust in her elaborate and ex-
       tended imagery, her fascination with time and memory,
       her use of incidental reflection about humanity, and
       especially in her style--"grave, a little formal,
       rather nineteenth century in its affection for the
       highly wrought complex sentence." The virtues of the
       novel are its "highly wrought and meticulous" style,
       its "carefully contrived" plot, and "its imaginative
       creation"; its defects are that the "characterization,
       though brilliant in its external finish, is not often
       very dense, and the big scenes and big emotions rarely
       come off with much real intensity."

G28   Young, Marguerite.   "The Dusty Interiors of Boston."
       Kenyon Review, 6 (Autumn 1944), 662–66.

       This   "provocative" and   "delightful"   novel has
       integrated many literary traditions and values,
       especially those of the English comedies of manners.

                    2.   THE MOUNTAIN LION

G29   Brown, Catherine Meredith.   "Farewell to Childhood."
       Saturday Review, 30 (1 March 1947), 15.

       "Miss Stafford writes with brilliance. Scene after
       scene is told with unforgettable care and tenuous
       entanglements are treated with wise subtlety."
       Portrait.

G30   Bullock, Florence Haxton.   "Study of Adolescent
       Suffering." *New York Herald Tribune Weekly Book
       Review,* 23 (2 March 1947), 3.

       This novel is a relentless and dazzlingly brilliant
       examination and vilification of "the painful state of
       being human and conscious."

G31 Carver, Catherine. "A Sign of Worth." *Partisan Review*, 14 (May-June 1947), 324-26.

This book is "so finely designed and so meticulously executed as to put to shame most current fiction." It is "on the whole so satisfactory that I want in this note to document only my praise of it." Especially praiseworthy are Stafford's ability to depict "the particularity of the external world," especially the "verbal quirks" of the different characters, and her style, which gives her perfect command of the internal landscape of her children and combines the interior and external realities to "tell a truth about the self."

G32 *Catholic World*, 165 (Aug. 1947), 476.

The moral of this "brilliantly written parable" is that "passion in all its mysterious ramifications can be overcome only by death and that death alone brings freedom to the soul."

G33 "Colorado Adventure." *Time*, 49 (10 March 1947), 100.

This is "a delicate, sharp story of childhood and adolescence," but the contrived ending makes for melodrama rather than tragedy. Portrait.

G34 Farrelly, John. "Fiction Chronicle." *New Republic*, 116 (24 March 1947), 34-35.

The protagonists' "mother is a minor masterpiece of ironic characterization"; Stafford's "use of the language is integral to her story and intentions to a degree rare in a time when most fiction is written in a slapdash approximate jargon and sluggish monologue."

G35 Fitzgerald, John. "The Children." *Nation*, 164 (5 April 1947), 399-400.

This book is "as good in its way as Elizabeth Bowen's 'Death of the Heart.' It is less polished, but it may be profounder in accounting for what the children suffer." Although "you read it with amusement, you will feel it aching in you like a tooth for days."

G36   Garrison, Winfred E.   *Christian Century*, 64 (2 July
      1947), 832.

      In this novel, Stafford "seems to feel unpleasantly
      superior to her characters, as though she were
      inviting the reader to join her in mildly ridiculing
      them.... Nevertheless, it is a novel of superior
      skill and ingenuity."

G37   Gelfant, Blanche H. "Reconsiderations: *The Mountain
      Lion*, by Jean Stafford." *New Republic*, 172 (10 May
      1975), 22-25.

      If "classic" is defined as "basic, typical and
      enduring," *ML* is a classic: "For it embodies our
      basic prejudices and enduring myths, and it represents
      our typical consciousness as Americans. If by classic
      we mean high quality, *The Mountain Lion* fits that
      definition too." Ralph's and Molly's loss of innocence
      is an allegory for America's loss of innocence, the
      West being the symbol of all hope. In the masculine
      myth of the West, there is no place for the female, as
      there is no place for Molly in the West of this novel.

G38   Hansen, Harry. "Letters and Life." *Survey Graphic*,
      36 (Aug. 1947), 449-50 [450].

      This book "is written with economy of language and
      with insight, but it remains a psychological study."

G39   Heilman, Robert B. "Four Novels." *Sewanee Review*, 55
      (Summer 1947), 483-92 [486-88].

      Stafford's characteristic excellencies are her
      "scrupulousness and modulation of style" and her
      ability to create single scenes through the use of
      "sensitively observed detail." Judged by the
      standards usually applied to the novel, *ML* is
      deficient in plot and character, but the book fits
      well into the genre of "the journal as fiction" and
      thus, should be judged on its own terms.

G40   Jackson, Joseph Henry.   San Francisco *Chronicle*, 10
      March 1947, p. 12.

      This is "as absorbing a novel of youth and adolescence
      as I've ever read" and by "an extraordinarily able
      writer."

G41   Jones, Howard Mumford. "A New Jean Stafford." *New York Times Book Review*, 2 March 1947, p. 5.

This second novel, though so different in setting, form, and style from her first, is "not a second-best novel," but is a "beautifully modeled tale."

G42   Kartmann, Ben. "Mountain Lion Saves Author by Neatly Solving All the Problems of Plot." *Chicago Sun Book Week*, 2 March 1947, p. 4.

This novel is so far inferior to her first one that one suspects "it is an earlier effort which Miss Stafford, for the sake of her literary prestige, should have kept locked in her trunk." The contrived ending is most objectionable.

G43   *Kirkus Reviews*, 15 (15 Feb. 1947), 104.

A "coldly analytical dismemberment of the mysteries of childhood and adolescence."

G44   *New Yorker*, 23 (8 March 1947), 97-98.

This is a "sharply focused study rather than a broad exploration of adolescence, written wittily, lucidly, and with great respect for the resources of the language."

G45   "Pair of Cubs." *Newsweek*, 29 (17 March 1947), 109-10.

The story is not a pretty one, "and some of the overtones are downright shocking, if the reader is not up on his Freud. But Miss Stafford tells it unsensationally, effectively, and subtly. Her book, despite signs of being a puffed-up short story, makes fresh and original reading." Portrait.

G46   "Paperbacks: New and Noteworthy." *New York Times Book Review*, 7 Aug. 1977, p. 33.

"Its riches are many--in language, in irony, in insights into life's ambiguities."

G47   Rago, Henry. *Commonweal*, 45 (4 April 1947), 618.

This is "an even finer novel than 'Boston Adventure,' though less brilliant." It has "a deeper richness of

child-myth and child-lore..., greater freedom of
perception and utterance," a "cleaner and more
athletic style," and a new dimension of irony, "for
now it is irony activated every moment by pity, the
most anguished pity."

G48   *Reprint Bulletin Book Reviews*, 22 (No. 4, 1977), 34.

Recommends the book "unreservedly and everywhere."

G49   Schorer, Mark. "The American Novel." *Kenyon Review*,
9 (Autumn 1947), 628-36 [635-36].

In this largely negative review of fourteen books,
Schorer concedes that *ML* is "certainly the best of the
books I have here discussed." He is especially
appreciative of Stafford's "demonstration of the first
importance of style in fiction," but he complains of
the structure of the novel, saying that the "novel
seems to be written only for the sake of the final
chapter."

G50   *U.S. Quarterly Book List*, 3 (June 1947), 140.

Stafford's "strength is in psychological analysis and
a control of suggestive imagery." Her defects are a
"somewhat loose" general structure, a sometimes
flatness of tone, and the "well-made" ending.

G51   West, Ray B., Jr. "A Note on American Fiction: 1947."
Western Review, 12 (Autumn 1947), 58-62 [58, 60-61].

Although this novel is not so good as *BA*, these "two
books (while not wholly successful) suggest the
possibility of a monumental work depicting the entire
panorama of American life."

G51a Wolcott, James. "Blowing Smoke into the Zeitgeist:
The Well-Deserved Resurrection of Jean Stafford."
Harper's, 266 (June 1983), 57-59.

The 1983 reissue of *ML* occasions this article on
Stafford's work as a whole, which Wolcott sees to be
characterized by her preoccupation with illness and
with the theme of abandonment. He attributes the
neglect of her work to her "long falling-off into
booze and scattered journalism," to her gender, and to
benign bad luck."

3. THE CATHERINE WHEEL

G52   *Booklist*, 48 (15 Feb. 1952), 197.

"Some readers may find the story morbid but the author's style and her ability to create atmosphere are compensating."

G53   *Bookmark* (The New York State Library), 11 (Feb. 1952), 108.

This is an "exquisitely written" novel "that will delight the discriminating reader."

G54   Bullock, Florence H.   "The Delicate Art of Jean Stafford."   *New York Herald Tribune Book Review*, 28 (13 Jan. 1952), 4.

Mostly descriptive, but praises Stafford for her ability to transmute "nuances of psychic experience into precise, inevitable prose."   Portrait.

G55   Engle, Paul.   "Jean Stafford's Stylistic Fire Glows in Her New Novel."   *Chicago Sunday Tribune Magazine of Books*, 13 Jan. 1952, p. 3.

This novel is "further proof of the fictional and psychological brilliance of the author."

G56   Fleischer, Lenore.   *Publisher's Weekly*, 189 (9 May 1966), 80.

This is a "sensitive and romantic novel."

G57   Flint, F. Cudworth.   "Fiction Chronicle."   *Sewanee Review*, 60 (Autumn 1952), 706-21 [709-10].

Mostly descriptive review of thirteen books of recent fiction.   Flint's major criticism of *CW* is Stafford's obtrusive superposition of the symbol of the Catherine wheel.

G58   Havighurst, Walter.   "Tragedy of Isolation."   *Saturday Review*, 35 (26 Jan. 1952), 11.

In this "superbly controlled" novel, Stafford, like
Hawthorne, is concerned with "the tragedy of human
isolation, the devious, painful, perilous struggle for
harmony and understanding. *The Catherine Wheel* is a
novel of great restraint and of great beauty."
Portrait.

G59   Hayes, Richard.   *Commonweal*, 55 (25 Jan. 1952), 404-
05.

"Like Mrs. Wharton, Miss Stafford has written a novel
to compel the imagination and nurture the mind; she
has also written one in which pity and terror combine
to reach us in the secret, irrational places of the
heart." Stafford writes, "as ever, with an eye to all
the implications and resources of the language," so
that "her endowments of style, sensibility and imagination, and her rare ability to invest experience with
moral value, diminish even the most distinguished of
her contemporaries."

G60   Howe, Irving. "Sensibility Troubles." *Kenyon Review*,
14 (Spring 1952), 345-48 [347-48].

This novel is not "nearly so good as its
predecessors": here, Stafford's "sensibility is so
voracious that it consumes the story." The prose of
this brilliant stylist "is so fine and frequently so
winning that it finally becomes a source of fascination in itself, undermining the matter it is supposed to reveal." In all three of her novels, there
is the same "virtuoso symbolism...; the mocking dupli-
cate of the major action, even some of the cleverness
of incidental observation," as well as her "proclivity
for violent endings."

G61   Hughes, Riley. *Catholic World*, 174 (March 1952), 469-
70.

"This book is an always elaborate, at times moving,
prose poem in which soft voices, sighing of money and
contentment speak of the ultimate tears of things."

G62   Jenkins, Elizabeth. "New Novels." *Manchester
Guardian*, 17 Oct. 1952, p. 4.

This is a "charmingly written and poignant book" in which the "pure, correct, and simple English" of the characters gives Englishmen a better opinion of educated American society than most American novels do.

G63 Jones, Ernest. "The Widening Circle." *Nation*, 174 (9 Feb. 1952), 136-37.

Although this is "the most engrossing unsuccessful novel" Jones has ever read, it fails because it tries to do too much and because of Stafford's ambiguous attitude toward her subjects: "She creates, constantly, the impression of seeing clear through everything she writes about to nothing at all."

G64 *Kirkus Reviews*, 19 (1 Dec. 1951), 681.

"A strangely involuted book, overwritten and complex, this is unlikely to enhance the reputation of the author of *Boston Adventure*."

G65 Libaire, Beatrice. *Library Journal*, 77 (15 Jan. 1952), 144.

"Recommended."

G66 McAleer, John. *Best Sellers*, 41 (Jan. 1982), 372.

"Her genre is the novel of manners," and Stafford's name is "properly linked" with this genre's greatest practicioners--Jane Austen, George Eliot, Henry James, and Edith Wharton.

G67 Martin, Hansford. "The Interrupted Tradition." *Western Review*, 17 (Winter 1953), 147-50.

CW is typical of a kind of fiction that has emerged in the Forties, its three most striking characteristics being "a preoccupation with the suprafunctional qualities of language, a reliance upon eventful and complicated plot, and a deliberate effort to exist in that realm which Peter Taylor has characterized as the province of the 'pure' story." A major fault of *CW* is its "melodramatic and fortuitous climax." After this climax, the reader feels tricked: "One realizes ... that the ornament and decoration of the language was just that, the long progress of sensibility, and of sensuous as well as moral perception, led only to a conjuror's device: and this device invalidates the passional problem of the novel and reveals the verbal furniture of the book to be its real excuse for being."

G68   Morris, Alice S. "When Hatred Breaks the Surface." *New York Times Book Review*, 13 Jan. 1952, p. 5.

"Miss Stafford is a novelist of such stature and of such brilliancy that it is difficult to track down why her story fails finally to be convincing, and so to be the moving experience one looks for.... Perhaps this is because at one point and another exaggeration spreads like a fascinating but fatal blight."

G69   Munn, L.S. "'The Catherine Wheel': Personal Problems." Springfield *Republican*, 9 March 1952, Sec. D, p. 8.

This novel, "for all its perceptiveness," is "over-subtle and disappointing," mainly because its substantive plot has not been integrated with its "distinctive" style.

G70   Phelps, Robert. "Fiction Parade." *New Republic*, 126 (10 March 1952), 21.

"As a sincere admirer of at least the first half of *Boston Adventure*, and having carefully reckoned the impertinence I am venturing, I suggest that Miss Stafford has now reached a crucial point in her career. Before getting too deep into her next novel, she should decide whether she wants to write honestly expressive, *unconcocted* literature, or very superior ladies-magazine serials. She has gifts enough to do either impressively; for her to go on preparing neither-fish-nor-fowl dishes seems a waste." The endings of all three of her novels are "preposterous."

G71   Rolo, Charles J. "Troubled Summer." *Atlantic*, 189 (Feb. 1952), 84.

Although this novel is "vastly superior to most current fiction," it is not so good as her first two novels: "despite beautiful writing and meticulous craftsmanship, the novel seems a bit lacking in force and in size."

G72   *Saturday Review*, 49 (27 Aug. 1966), 30.

      "The prose as usual is impeccable."

G73   Scott, J.D.   "New Novels."   *New Statesman & Nation*, 44
      (25 Oct. 1952), 489.

      CW is "a novel of great accomplishment."

G74   "Searchings and Findings."   *Times Literary Supplement*,
      24 Oct. 1952, p. 689.

      This novel, in spite of the "subtlety" of Stafford's
      technique and "the fine texture of her writing" marks
      "a decline in originality," because the book is so
      reminiscent of the Eudora Welty manner.

G75   "Stafford's   Studied   Prose."   *Newsweek*,   39   (14 Jan.
      1952), 87.

      "The prose of Jean Stafford ... is so polished and
      worked over that it sometimes seems surprising that it
      can communicate anything at all."   This novel "appears
      almost to have been written in reverse, not with a
      style polished to tell a story, but with life fixed up
      to meet the requirements of style."   Portrait.

G76   *U.S. Quarterly Book Review*, 8 (June 1952), 139.

      "Subtle and moving," this narrative is characterized
      by "richness of texture" and "increasing psychological
      tension."   However, the "very virtuosity of the author
      ... leads her to make too much of an essentially minor
      story...."

C77   Wales,   Ruth.   "'Things   Unreal   or   Disappointing.'"
      Christian Science Monitor, 24 Jan. 1952, p. 11.

      Although Stafford is a "mature craftsman" and the
      action of the novel is developed "with tender com-
      passion and insight," the world of the novel seems
      unreal, every character a caricature.

G78   West, Anthony.   "Books: 'Parsifal' in Modern Dress."
      New Yorker, 27 (12 Jan. 1952), 75-76, 78, 81 [76, 78,
      81].

This is an excellent story "of misunderstanding and
the width that divides children from their elders."
However, Stafford's tendency to overly detailed
descriptions interferes with the emotional immediacy
of her story.

G79   "Where Cuts Don't Bleed." *Time*, 59 (14 Jan. 1952),
       94.

In this new novel by "probably the best young prose
writer in the U.S ... the manner is still fine, but
the matter is thinner than ever." Although Stafford's
prose is "gracious, sensuous and only occasionally
self-conscious," its very delicacy and grace cause the
reader to be shocked, but not moved, by the tragic
ending. Portrait.

G80   *Wisconsin Library Bulletin*, 48 (March 1952), 95.

"An excellent psychological study."

G81   Wolcott, James. *Esquire*, 97 (March 1982), 136.

In this review of the reprint of *CW* by Ecco Press, as
part of its "Neglected Books of the 20th Century"
series, Wolcott says that he does not understand how
the book ever came to be neglected: "it beats hollow
nearly every novel published by a 'name' author in the
post-World War II era." Stafford is "one of the truly
great underrateds."

G82   Yaffe, James. "Outstanding Novels." *Yale Review*,
       n.s.41 (Spring 1952), vi-xx [x].

Yaffee evaluates several novelists according to their
"ability to create characters who convince the reader
that they are alive, and to present them in dramatic,
vigorous, believable situations." He finds *CW* to be a
"triumph of literary manner over characterization,"
and charges Stafford, in the second half of the book,
with engaging "in a kind of pseudo-poetic 'fine'
writing," which destroys the clarity of her characters.

G83   Young, Vernon. "Ghosts and Flesh, Vinegar and Wine:
       Ten Recent Novels." *New Mexico Quarterly*, 22 (Autumn
       1952), 322-30 [325-26, 330].

Stafford's subject here is, as always, "that of Loss, which she expresses in an extraordinarily leisured, measured and sometimes clotted) prose that, for me, always misses the passionate center." She writes "in the English tradition of country-house literature, with the knowledge of an interior decorator and the memory of an elephant." This novel gives the impression that "she is a writer of exceptionally subtle craft struggling, none too fiercely, to break through a stained-glass window of the mind."

4. CHILDREN ARE BORED ON SUNDAY

G84 Baro, Gene. "The Several Worlds of Jean Stafford." *New York Herald Tribune Book Review*, 29 (10 May 1953), 3.

Stafford's major strength is the "compelling believability" of her characters, the result of her ability to show the "significant rapport and reciprocal influence between these characters and their environments." Although Stafford's vision is essentially an intellectual one, "it does not overwhelm or needlessly complicate her materials." Portrait.

G85 *Booklist*, 49 (15 May 1953), 304.

"The writer transcribes the dilemmas of her stranded persons in a mannered and Jamesian prose."

G86 *Bookmark* (The New York State Library), 12 (June 1953), 209.

These stories "evidence her delicacy of feeling and exquisite choice of words."

G87 Engle, Paul. "Subtlety and Power in Collection of Short Stories by Skilful Novelist." *Chicago Sunday Tribune Magazine of Books*, 10 May 1953, p. 2.

Stafford's novels and stories "have been among the best that have been produced in this country," chiefly because of her "firm imaginativeness of language."

One of her recurring themes is "the person who turns
out, in the most casual way, to be the opposite of
what he first seemed." The most moving story of all
is "The Interior Castle." Portrait.

G88   Hay, John. "Interim Struggle." *Commonweal*, 58 (15
      May 1953), 158-59.

These stories seem "stifled, muted, unrealized, by the
very effort in which they were conceived. They were
very skillfully written. But the heart is so often
stopped in them, the extravagance kicked in the teeth,
the main question not answered. Heart, don't cry too
hard, they seem to say; the outcome is impossible."
The best of these stories is "The Interior Castle."

G89   Jones, Howard Mumford. "Memories of Metaphysics."
      Saturday Review, 36 (9 May 1953), 19.

Although Stafford is "an extraordinarily perceptive
talent," and has "masterly control over language as an
instrument," she has a tendency to become absorbed in
the technological aspects of writing, which perhaps
"springs from a kind of terror--terror at the abysses
of human nature itself, its unpredictability, its
self-deception, the little role which rationality has
in its operation." Portrait.

G90   *Kirkus Reviews*, 21 (15 April 1953), 270.

"At her best in this medium, her stories have a
certain cold brilliance and an implacable finality."

G91   Martin, Hansford. "Four Volumes of Short Stories: An
      Irreverent Review." *Western Review*, 18 (Winter 1954),
      172-74.

In this review of Stafford's *CABS*, J.D. Salinger's
Nine Stories, Ray Bradbury's *The Golden Apples of the
Sun*, and Budd Schulberg's *Some Faces in the Crowd*,
Martin says that Stafford "is undoubtedly the only
serious writer" of the four. However, Stafford's main
literary problem is the "disjunction of form and
content." Her words exert "an undue weight ... upon a
too frail substance of subject."

G92   *Nation,* 176 (6 June 1953), 488.

In these "excellent tales," Stafford "has come to
balance the virtuosity of her talent by a consistent
regard for those who have been exploited by the bru-
talities of civilization as well as by the aberrations
of psychobiology."

G93   *Newsweek,* 41 (11 May 1953), 111.

"A Country Love Story" is the best of these stories.
Portrait.

G94   Peden, William. "A Bleak, Sad World." *New York Times
Book Review,* 10 May 1953, p. 5.

Most of these stories "center around an individual who
is struggling to maintain his identity and self-
respect in the face of some abnormality or accident of
fate which alienates him from his fellows." Although
Stafford's world "is a bleakly inhibited one, into
which sunlight and fresh air seldom penetrate, it is
honestly observed and superbly recorded."

G95   Pickrel, Paul. "Outstanding Novels." *Yale Review,*
n.s.42 (Summer 1953), vi-xvi [xii].

Most of these stories are "overwrought, both in an
emotional sense and in the sense that they are decked
out in too much verbal embroidery." Some, like "The
Echo and the Nemesis," are impressive; but others,
like "The Bleeding Heart," are "artificial, made-up,
and literary."

G96   *U.S. Quarterly Book Review,* 9 (Sept. 1953), 300-01.

"Ten subtle and rather fragile documents of human
loneliness." Stafford's least successful area is
"that of the sophisticate world, where brittleness of
subject is added to customary brittleness of style."
Her stories are "without sentimental garnish, perhaps
equally without the warmth of human sympathy."

G97   Walbridge, Earle F. *Library Journal,* 78 (1 May 1953),
810.

These stories are "all guaranteed to leave you
thoroughly depressed." Stafford "casts a cold eye,
not to say a jaundiced one on her fellow
creatures.... Well-written, and all that."

G98   "The Weather of the Heart." *Time*, 61 (11 May 1953),
      118.

A short story should probe in the remote corners of
the heart, preferably a "broken, guilty or sick" one,
and Stafford is "one of the finest heart specialists
now practicing in U.S. short fiction." These
stories, characterized by "a somberly muted tone of
helpless rage that the things she writes about can
be," are "ten small monuments to minor tragedy. Her
trouble is that she cannot make them seem major."
Consequently, her stories poke at the heart, but they
never make it miss a beat. Portrait.

G99   *Wisconsin Library Bulletin*, 49 (May 1953), 128.

"Witty but not too wise, gently ribbing and never
disdainful or scornful, the essays [sic] are urbane,
bucolic, introspective and pathetic. One thing they
never are, tiresome."

           5. A WINTER'S TALE (*IN NEW SHORT NOVELS*)

G100 *Booklist*, 50 (1 April 1954), 297.

Brief, mainly descriptive review.

G101 *Bookmark* (The New York State Library), 13 (April
      1954), 158.

Brief, mainly descriptive review.

G102 Calisher, Hortense. "A Form In-Between." *New York
      Times Book Review*, 14 March 1954, pp. 5, 19.

Although *WT* is written with distinction, it "reads
like brilliant, haphazard notes for a novel."

G103   Coppinger, John M. *Best Sellers*, 14 (15 April 1954),
        12-13.

        WT is the best of the four short novels. It is
        "fictive expertise: a fine example of a craftswoman
        who holds all the elements of her story in firm hands
        (though there is a questionable slip at the end) and
        who uses words with miserly economy but admirable
        efficiency."

G104   *Kirkus Reviews*, 22 (1 Jan. 1954), 10.

        Brief, mainly descriptive review.

G105   *New Yorker*, 30 (20 Feb. 1954), 102-03.

        Stafford is "a commanding writer whose poise,
        intelligence, and devastating humor turn her story of
        a long-ago love affair into a small, but complete and
        steady, illumination."

G106   Peden, William. "Quatrefoil Modern." *Saturday
        Review*, 37 (6 March 1954), 17.

        This is a "small gem from one of our most gifted
        writers"; it is "not Miss Stafford's best, but very
        good indeed."

G107   Philbrick, Richard. "Increasing the Popularity of the
        Short Novel." *Chicago Sunday Tribune Magazine of
        Books*, 21 March 1954, 14.

        "These works are highly entertaining pieces of
        fiction."

G108   Quinn, Patrick F. *Commonweal*, 60 (9 April 1954), 19-
        20.

        WT is "the most richly embroidered" of the four
        stories, "and by all odds the strangest."

G109   Rolo, Charles J. *Atlantic*, 193 (April 1954), 88.

        Brief, mainly descriptive review.

G110   Rosenberger, Coleman. "Neglected Stepchildren of
        Literature." *New York Herald Tribune Book Review*, 14
        March 1954, p. 7.

Because of its almost clinical detachment, *WT* "makes
little attempt to involve the reader's sympathetic
concern for the characters--running the risk of losing
the reader's interest as well--but on the level of
technical virtuosity it is perhaps the most
accomplished of the four short novels here."

G111   San Francisco *Chronicle, This World Magazine*, 8 Aug.
       1954, p. 20.

       "Disparate in tone and feeling," these four short
       novels "have in common their almost equal excellence."

G112   *Wisconsin Library Bulletin*, 50 (May 1954), 135-36.

       Each of the novels in this "excellent collection" is
       "typical of its author's best efforts--at least in
       each author's eyes."

G113   "Worth the Money." *Time*, 63 (15 Feb. 1954), 100, 102,
       104.

       WT is "expertly written." Portrait.

6. STORIES
(With John Cheever, Daniel Fuchs, and William Maxwell)

G114   *Booklist*, 52 (1 Jan. 1957), 225.

       These short stories "are similar in attention to
       craftsmanship and style.... For the sophisticated
       reader."

G115   Burnette, Frances. *Library Journal*, 81 (1 Dec. 1956),
       2846-47.

       "Recommended for large fiction collections."

G116   *Chicago Review*, 10 (Winter 1957), 98.

       "The Liberation" is the weakest of these stories, but
       "Bad Characters" is the best. Stafford's stories are
       "an adult's L.M. Montgomery." All the stories in this

collection "suffer from an oppressive and monotonous psychoanalytic orientation."

G117 Engle, Paul. "Superb, Brief Tales by Four American Writers." *Chicago Sunday Tribune Magazine of Books*, 23 Dec. 1956, p. 5.

Stafford's unique quality is her "remarkable feeling for the baffled child in a blunted adult world." Her "steady comic sense" saves "her stories from dullness or gloom." Stafford, unlike "the usual European lady writer," has "none of that oversensitivity which disfigures even the best female writers across the ocean."

G118 Hogan, William. San Francisco *Chronicle*, 6 Dec. 1956, p. 25.

Although all four of the writers here are craftsmen, Stafford is "perhaps the artist of the company." She is "a fine stylist with haunting quality, who, incidentally, is the author of two of the most underrated novels of our time, 'The Catherine Wheel' and 'The Mountain Climber' [sic]."

G119 *Kirkus Reviews*, 24 (1 Oct. 1956), 764.

Brief, mostly descriptive review.

G120 Martinez, Ramona Maher. *New Mexico Quarterly*, 26 (Winter 1956-57), 406-07.

Comments specifically on two of the five stories by Stafford: "The Liberation" and "Maggie Meriwether's Rich Experience," the latter of which she finds "razor-sharp, inimitable Stafford in many ways, but lamentably, often razor-thin."

G121 Nordell, Rod. "With 'a Kind of Hollow Good Cheer.'" *Christian Science Monitor*, 6 Dec. 1956, p. 11.

"Miss Stafford, who is the most generously represented, has a saving irony that suggests she sees both sides of any given coin. She can deal sensitively with the despairing, but she has a sense of humor, especially welcome in this company...."

G122   Peden, William.   "Four Cameos."   *Saturday Review*, 39
       (8 Dec. 1956), 15-16, 52.

       "Jean   Stafford's   success   in   depicting   misfits,
       societal and otherwise, is extraordinary."   The best
       of the stories is "The Liberation."

G123   Perrine,   Laurence.   "Realism   Plus   Symbolism."
       Southwest Review, 42 (Spring 1957), 166-67.

       "The book is held together by a sympathy of subject
       and method, for each of the authors works in the
       realistic tradition using symbolic overtones, and each
       is concerned with the tensions of modern American
       life, at the individual, the family, and the community
       levels."   Perrine comments specifically on Stafford's
       "The Liberation" and "In the Zoo."

G124   Sullivan, Richard.   "A Talented Quartet."   *New York
       Times Book Review*, 23 Dec. 1956, p. 10.

       Brief, mostly descriptive review.

G125   *Time*, 68 (3 Dec. 1956), 106-07.

       Stafford is "the most accomplished craftsman of the
       group," although her work is marred "by a truly
       feminine absorption in detail so that sometimes she
       seems to be writing for visitors from Mars."

                       7.   ARABIAN NIGHTS

G126   *Christian Science Monitor*, 15 Nov. 1962, Sec. B, p. 8.

       Brief, mostly descriptive review.

G127   "In Modern Dress."   *Times Literary Supplement*, 23 Nov.
       1962, p. 905.

       Brief, descriptive review.

G128   Lask,   Thomas.   "Repeat   Performances   (Juvenile
       Division)."   *New York Times Book Review*, Part 2, 11
       Nov. 1962, pp. 62-63.

Brief mention of the publication of this book in a
review article on "books that generations have prized
and which appear in very attractive dress."

8. ELEPHI: THE CAT WITH THE HIGH I.Q.

G129 Bannon, Barbara A.   *Publisher's Weekly*, 190 (29 Aug.
      1966), 351.

"How marvelously Miss Stafford understands her cats!"

G130 Bruce, Jeannette.   "New Books--Jean Stafford's Feline
      Hero."   San Francisco *Chronicle, This World Magazine*,
      16 Sept. 1962, p. 35.

Stafford "has written an amusing trifle about her pet
with whom she and her husband, A.J. Liebling, share
their home in New York."

G131 Buell, Ellen Lewis.   *New York Times Book Review*, 16
      Sept. 1962, p. 38.

"Occasionally Miss Stafford slips into the overcute
but she makes up for that with her amusing sketches of
the contemporary scene, her quick eye for people, and
her affectionate, unillusioned knowledge of cats."

G132 Johnson, Siddie Joe.   *Library Journal*, 87 (15 Dec.
      1962), 47.

"Delightful story with delightful illustrations about
a delightful cat....   Recommended for the very
sophisticated child and adult cat lovers."

9. BAD CHARACTERS

G133 Anderson, Polly G.   *Library Journal*, 89 (15 Oct.
      1964), 3975.

"A new compassion and good-natured humor appear occasionally alongside the author's well-known caustic wit, bitterness and jaundiced view of humanity."

G134 Baro, Gene. "Breaking Out of Isolation." *New York Times Book Review*, 11 Oct. 1964, p. 4.

"Jean Stafford is surely one of our best writers. She makes the English language a weapon or a wand. She can build solidly in the tradition of Hawthorne and James. She can manage the deceptive simplicities and sleight-of-hand of colloquial style. Dry wit or zany humor are well within her range. She is an impeccable social observer, with a sense of telling detail."

G135 Barrett, William. *Atlantic*, 214 (Dec. 1964), 152.

Stafford's most interesting characters are children. This collection does not contain the best of Stafford's stories because they are lacking in insight, though not in "sheer competence and proficiency."

G136 *Booklist*, 61 (1 Nov. 1964), 249.

"With her usual penetration and craftsmanship Miss Stafford lays before the reader the dreams and loneliness of childhood, the groping of youth, and some adult tyrannies."

G137 Casey, Florence. "'Look What I've Done for You.'" *Christian Science Monitor*, 3 Dec. 1964, Sec. B, p. 7.

Although these stories have the style and "highly polished subjectivism" typical of *New Yorker* stories, "Miss Stafford is one of the few members of that club who manages to keep one eye on the macrocosm while twiddling with the microscope."

G138 *Choice*, 2 (March 1965), 24.

"Ten penetrating, often witty stories by one of our best fiction writers.... Indispensable for any modern American literature collection." *WT* is the most brilliant.

G139 Copeland, Edith. *Books Abroad*, 39 (Summer 1965), 351-52.

These stories are told "with warmth and humor, and an extraordinary sense of reality."

G140 Corodimas, Peter. *Best Sellers*, 24 (15 Oct. 1964), 285-86.

This collection is "a substantial improvement" over her first collection in that most of the severity and pessimism of *CABS* here give way to hope.

G141 Crews, Frederick C. "Private Lives, Public Lives." *New York Review of Books*, 3 (5 Nov. 1964), 13-15 [14].

These stories are distinguished "by a good-natured, low-keyed humanity," but perhaps they are "too relaxed to be engaging," lacking as they are in any sense of personal urgency.

G142 Curley, Thomas. *Commonweal*, 81 (19 Feb. 1965), 673.

"Her intelligence is acute, her heart is in the right place and she writes well," but she "so manages her characters that you always like and dislike the ones she likes and dislikes." Curley comments specifically on *WT*.

G143 Davenport, Guy. "Tough Characters, Solid Novels." *National Review*, 17 (26 Jan. 1965), 66.

"The ten stories of this collection are all excellent and do not easily fade from the memory. They are also very wise."

G144 Hicks, Granville. "Slices of Life in an Age of Anxiety." *Saturday Review*, 47 (17 Oct. 1964), 33-34.

"These are all good stories with important themes, vivid characterization, and excellent craftsmanship."

G145 Hill, William B. *America*, 111 (28 Nov. 1964), 719.

The style of these stories is, "to say the least, impressive."

G146 Kistner, Madge. "Bad Characters." *North American Review*, n.s.2 (Spring 1965), 57-58.

"In each story she creates a memorable character
although the creation and the story occasionally have
no strong connection.... One method Stafford uses to
delineate her distinctive characters is the accumulation of revealing detail." *WT* is the masterpiece of
the collection.

G147   Mazzaro, Jerome L.   "Remembrance of Things Proust."
       Shenandoah, 16 (Summer 1965), 114-17.

Both Stafford and Proust have "the remarkable
tendencies to stop time and in time's stoppage to
create memorable characters." The limitations of
Stafford's Proustian approach are oversimplification
and an overemphasis on manner--style and characterization. Nevertheless, her "prose style is remarkable
and withstands any comparison with Henry James's
prose; her grasp of situation is often flawless; and
her characters, even when unimportant, emerge fully-
drawn." Because of her overemphasis and oversimplification, "the writing in *Bad Characters* does not seem
major." Furthermore, "her fiction seems unaffected by
the major social, intellectual, artistic, and philosophical movements since the mid-forties."

G148   Oates, Joyce Carol.   "Notions Good and Bad."   *Kenyon
       Review*, 27 (Winter 1965), 175-80 [177-78].

This book is "a triumph of style and imagination. The
writing is elegant without being pretentious; most
importantly, it is always suited precisely to the
rhythm of the emotions she wants to express.... But
Miss Stafford's real gift is her ability to conjure up
a world we believe in.... These stories are achievements of art, short-story writing at its finest."

G149   Perry, Eleanor.   "Who Remembers That Fine Fellow,
       What's-His-Name?" *Book Week*, 11 Oct. 1964, pp. 6, 21.

WT is "a beautifully constructed novella and the best
piece in this new collection." Stafford is "one of
the finest writers publishing today, is a genius at
creating 'bad' characters"; the good ones all "suffer
from a paralysis of will, they are vitiated by
guilt. Their destinies are solved by external
events."

G150 Poore, Charles. "Books of the Times." New York *Times*, 13 Oct. 1964, p. 41.

These stories exhibit "razory wit and exuberance."

G151 Pryce-Jones, Alan. New York *Herald Tribune*, 15 Oct. 1964, p. 25.

Stafford is "an extremely feminine good writer." These tales are told in language which "lilts and bubbles." She can also "draw blood when she wishes."

G152 *Saturday Review*, 47 (3 Oct. 1964), 38.

Brief, mostly descriptive review.

G153 "Stories in Short." *Times Literary Supplement*, 28 Oct. 1965, p. 964.

As good as these stories are, they nevertheless illustrate an attitude characteristic of stories published in the *New Yorker*: "there is a self-consciously dry, wry precision about Miss Stafford's style, as though, while avoiding the least suggestion of boring pedantry, it was essential to make clear that writer and reader share an intellectual background, share a sophisticated appreciation of the nuances of both style and behaviour infinitely more rarified than the average American."

G154 Taylor, Griffin. "Time and the Annihilators: Five Views of Seeking and Finding at Mid-Century." *Sewanee Review*, 73 (Autumn 1965), 736-47 [741-43].

Stafford "has a special gift for telling tales of delicate fantasy that are at the same time mercilessly satirical." Praiseworthy are her "studious detachment" and "the stateliness of her prose, which is at times elaborate, even fastidiously ornate." *WT* is the "most moving and most powerful" of these stories.

G155 *Time*, 84 (23 Oct. 1964), 116.

WT is the "most compelling" of these stories. "Other stories concern the casualties of child vs. parent warfare, of which there are few keener combat correspondents than the author."

G156   Tracy, Honor.   "Jean Stafford's Human Zoo."   *New*
       Republic, 151 (31 Oct. 1964), 22-23.

       Stafford has "all a writer needs--observation,
       sympathy, humor, a great eye for a theme, a lively way
       with words, and the capacity to break fresh ground."
       However, she frequently uses the "devices and con-
       ventions that belong properly in a glossy magazine."

G157   Wardle, I.   "Under Eastern Eyes."   *Observer* (London),
       19 Sept. 1965, p. 29.

       Stafford is "a writer with a sharp set of claws."
       However, she has "plenty of unaffected charm and
       sympathy which lift her book well above the merely
       professional level."

                    10.   A MOTHER IN HISTORY

G158   Baxter, Annette K.   "Mom Talks."   *New York Times Book*
       Review, 13 March 1966, pp. 16, 18.

       Stafford brings her "well-honed Jamesian sensibility"
       to the examination of the personality of Mrs. Oswald.

G159   *Booklist*, 62 (15 March 1966), 685.

       "A chilling character sketch almost entirely a self-
       portrait by Marguerite Oswald, the mother of
       Lee Harvey Oswald....   A pitiless reportorial
       exercise...."

G160   Casey, Florence.   "Her 'Why?' Gets No Answer."
       Christian Science Monitor, 3 March 1966, p. 5.

       "'Why?' The 'historical mother' voices the plaintive
       word again and again. Miss Stafford offers no ex-
       plicit response, but provides some insight into those
       personalities who seek, half-consciously, the enmity
       of the world--and receive it."

G161   Christopher, Michael.   "The New Books: Capote,
       Fielding, Oswald, Kung."   *U.S. Catholic*, 31 (April
       1966), 62.

This is "an unfortunate book" whose appeal "is to morbidity." Mrs. Oswald deserves pity and privacy, and Stafford's injection "of herself and her own personality into the report is irritating and offensive. Mrs. Oswald is perfectly able to damn herself; snide remarks and attempts to further prejudice the reader are inexcusable." This book is a disservice to Stafford's readers and to her reputation.

G162   Dole, Grace Fuller. *Library Journal*, 91 (15 April 1966), 2051.

"Recommended for public libraries only."

G163   Fleischer, Lenore. *Publisher's Weekly*, 190 (15 Aug. 1966), 68.

This is a "brief but absolutely chilling portrait" of Mrs. Oswald. "Miss Stafford not only makes every word of her portrait count, she also manages to get across the significance of the things she *doesn't* say."

G164   Fremont-Smith, Eliot. "How Oswald Happened." New York *Times*, 115 (23 Feb. 1966), 37.

This is a "shocked and shocking book," with Stafford's shock betraying itself "in occasional little cruelties of thought and tone."

G165   Gardner, John. "An Invective Against Mere Fiction." *Southern Review*, n.s.3 (Spring 1967), 444-67 [448-49].

In this "tasteless book," Stafford is to be criticized for her superciliousness, for being "emotionally trivial," and for selling out to "the snobbish, complacent, chattering ladies' magazines."

G166   Gelhorn, Martha. "American Mom." *Books and Bookmen*, 12 (Oct. 1966), 59, 82.

"Perhaps Miss Stafford puts herself in the picture too often, as if to remind herself that she is still there, still sane; and this is a journalistic error."

G167   Hicks, Granville.   "Mother of the Accused." *Saturday Review*, 49 (5 March 1966), 33-34.

Stafford "has given us an unforgettable picture of what is (I'm afraid) an unforgettable woman."

G168   Hodgson, Godfrey.   "Mrs. O. and Miss S." *Observer* (London), 11 Sept. 1966, p. 26.

"Miss Stafford carries detachment to the brink of contempt and sometimes beyond it, punctuating the torrent of Mrs. Oswald's naive self-revelation with cruel little touches of the whip.... This is a book about two women, and of the two, I find Miss Stafford, with her knowing New York superiority and her lack of human sympathy, quite as chilling as the other."

G169   Holzhauer, Jean.   *Commonweal*, 84 (13 May 1966), 233-34.

"Striving for objectivity, carefully crediting Mrs. Oswald with all her plausible abilities, Miss Stafford clearly remains a sensitive intelligence embarked on a distasteful assignment." Yet this book seems to have little purpose other than those of "profit and curiosity-seeking."

G170   Hughes, Riley. *Columbia*, 46 (May 1966), 40-41.

This is "another example of the journalist art of profile."

G171   Jackson, Katherine G.   *Harper's*, 232 (April 1966), 123.

Stafford's reactions as novelist-reporter to Mrs. Oswald's words contribute significantly to the "horrible poignancy" of the book.

G172   *Kirkus Reviews*, 33 (15 Dec. 1965), 1260.

The book is "fascinating to read, implacable in its inferences and impeccable in its presentation."

G173   La Rosa, Barbara. *America*, 114 (19 March 1966), 390, 394.

This is "primarily a running narration by Mrs. Oswald, with some asides and apt comments by Miss Stafford."

G174   Larner, Jeremy. "Oswald's Mother." *Dissent*, 13 (May-June 1966), 330.

The dialogue of Mrs. Oswald is so repelling and disturbing that Stafford's commentary "apparently designed to demonstrate the writer's superiority to her subject," is unnecessary.

G175   McCabe, Bernard. *New Blackfriars*, 48 (Jan. 1967), 222-23.

Stafford's scoring off Mrs. Oswald is tasteless. Her "brittle, even fun-poking hostility.... seems an inadequate response" and "not very interesting." Mrs. Oswald surely is "pitiable as well as horrible."

G176   "Mama Oswald." *Newsweek*, 67 (28 Feb. 1966), 92A-94.

This book is "a masterpiece of character study and a gem of personal journalism." Stafford comments about writing the book that "there were only two split seconds when I felt any pity at all for her—and I am generally a patsy."

G177   Mannes, Marya. "Woman Behind the Gun." *Book Week*, 27 Feb. 1966, p. 4.

Mannes surveys the outraged reader reaction to the portion that appeared in *McCall's*. She defends Stafford, who "hardly speaks at all," and sees the book as "a triumph of control not only over material but over the writer's emotions."

G178   Miller, Karl. "Moving Around." *New Statesman*, 72 (30 Sept. 1966), 486.

This is a "writer's book"; it is "preoccupied with the author's own travail and discomfort."

G179   "Mother Knows Best?" *Time*, 87 (8 April 1966), 112.

This is "by far her most thoroughly unpleasant book—perhaps the most abrasively unpleasant book in recent years—and it required no writing talent at all." Portrait.

G180   Peterson, Clarence.   *Chicago Sunday Tribune Books Today*, 3 (2 Oct. 1966), 7.

        Brief, mostly descriptive review.

G181   Pryce-Jones, Alan.   New York *Herald Tribune*, 8 March 1966, p. 23.

        "As a straight reporter, Miss Stafford is beyond praise.   Where she goes beyond reporting she is sometimes too ready with a biased verdict."

G182   Richard, Paul.   "Mother's Day in Fort Worth."   *New Republic*, 154 (26 March 1966), 22-23.

        Why did Stafford publish this interview with Oswald's mother?   "It makes a petty and altogether disagreeable little book."

G183   *Saturday Review*, 49 (29 Oct. 1966), 35.

        This is "an artful reconstruction of the author's weird conversations with Marguerite Oswald," who is "as possessed as any fictional female" Stafford has ever created.

G184   Stern, Karl.   "Mediocrity's Monstrous Issue."   *Critic*, 24 (June-July 1966), 62-64.

        "Miss Stafford writes with that elegant sparseness and controlled irony which we have come to admire in all her work."

G185   *Virginia Quarterly Review*, 42 (Summer 1966), civ.

        Stafford has been accused of relying excessively on her tape-recorded conversations with Mrs. Oswald, but no one "but a skilled and sensitive novelist could have achieved this record, this insight."

G186   Waltz, J.R.   "An Arrogant, Endless Monolog."   *Chicago Sunday Tribune Books Today*, 3 (27 Feb. 1966), 6.

        "This is *not* a book about the mother of Lee Harvey Oswald.   It is a book *by* her, since it is compounded primarily of monologs....   It is a non-book wholly

worthless except to those who may wish" to find out
whether Mrs. Oswald is sane.

11. THE COLLECTED STORIES

G187 Anderson, Polly G. *Library Journal*, 94 (15 Feb.
1969), 782.

"In this collection Miss Stafford's virtues of
clarity, well-chosen words, perception of people and
places almost disappear under the sheer numbers of
bad-tempered, eccentric, pitiful old women and the
emotions of loneliness, frustration, aimlessness,
terror and despair."

G188 *Antioch Review*, 29 (Spring 1969), 109.

This collection "by one of our finest
storytellers.... testifies to a delicate but tough
sensibility that is uniquely special for the way it
observes, remembers, evokes, thinks, and discovers."
It is "limited only because it attempts so rarely to
set off reverberations that are really deep, really
moving."

G189 *Atlantic Monthly*, 246 (July 1980), 86.

The re-issue of this volume is fortunate "for
Stafford's wit, craftsmanship, and humanity are
reminders of the worlds that this genre can
create.... A sense of life's disappointments is
everywhere felt in these stories, which often have
autobiographical overtones."

G190 Axthelm, Pete. *Newsweek*, 73 (3 March 1969), 86B.

Stafford's technical virtuosity is such that this
collection could become a textbook for students of
short fiction. Stafford, along with Katherine
Mansfield and Eudora Welty, is "one of a group of
modern female writers who share an intensely
introspective, feminine sensibility." In the Stafford

world, "love is a rare commodity.... Her vision is
sympathetic and yet ultimately bleak."

G191   Bailey, Paul. "A Mini-Proust." *Observer* (London), 21
       June 1970, p. 30.

       Although Staffod is not well-known in England, she
       "certainly deserves to be." She is like Proust, "a
       mini-Proust," in her appreciation of "the values of
       the homespun approach to life."

G192   *Book World*, Washington (D.C.) *Post*, 29 June 1969, p.
       8.

       "Impeccably written stories, droll, elegaic and
       alarming, about dislocated individuals."

G193   *Book World*, Washington (D.C.) *Post*, 7 Dec. 1969, p.
       12.

       "Stories--droll, delicate, cruel--ranging over some
       twenty years by a master of the short-story form;
       their subject, a very American sort of isolation."

G194   *Book World*, Washington (D.C.) *Post*, 6 April 1980, p.
       9.

       Stafford is "one of the best modern American short
       story writers, comparable to Katherine Anne Porter,
       Peter Taylor, and Eudora Welty."

G195   *Booklist*, 65 (15 April 1969), 943.

       "Thirty masterly stories ... that reaffirm Stafford's
       superb control over the genre."

G196   *Choice*, 6 (Sept. 1969), 821.

       "Recommended for literature students and the general
       reading public."

G197   Davenport, Guy. *New York Times Book Review*, 16 Feb.
       1969, pp. 1, 40.

       Stafford's major theme is that "man is a double
       prisoner"--of society and self. In many stories, the
       characters are imprisoned in an institution, and "all

of them study the inescapable confinement of the
self." In these stories, "The American woman at all
ages is the crucial center. She is the medium through
which tradition and manners survive; she must both
build and inhabit the prison." By looking "with such
patient scrutiny ... at the inner life of woman, Miss
Stafford has gone to the very quick of American
life." Portrait.

G198 Dickstein, Morris. "Domesticated Modernism." *New
Republic*, 160 (8 March 1969), 25-27.

Although Stafford "has a special if fragile vision of
her own," the influence of James, Dickens, Mark Twain,
Mann, and E.M. Forster are apparent in these
stories. "Like many other American writers of the
40's and 50's she inhabits a form that might be
described as domesticated modernism. Her stories do
not primarily focus on men and events; instead an
atmosphere is created, a situation explored; we are
granted not a conclusive action or denouement but only
the significant word, the telltale gesture, the small
illumination." Her fiction is "so gracefully professional, so eloquent and disciplined.... But in the
more serious stories, where deeper insight is demanded, style tends to expose itself as *mere* style."

G199 Edelstein, Arthur. "Art and Artificiality in Some
Recent Fiction." *Southern Review*, 9 (Summer 1973),
736-44 [736-38].

The best of Stafford's stories "breathe that air of
gentility which is her signature." Nevertheless,
"these stories are not genteel, for they slice unhesi-
tatingly through that protective skin of Victorian
furniture, rare crystal, tins of foie gras, and
discussions of 'the servant situation' into the pulpy
underlayer of folly--but with a grace that stays the
cutting edge one layer short of cynicism, at the
precise depth where all is exposed and nothing
destroyed."

G200 Hentoff, Margot. *Vogue*, 154 (July 1969), 56.

Stafford's stories make us realize how different is
our world today from that of the forties and fifties,
when most of these stories appeared. "There is often

an icy privacy about Jean Stafford's work which is
perversely warming. One is drawn back to a time when
we were a nation of cranky individualists bound
together by conventions rather than a 'liberated' mass
looking for a home. Here, one goes to one's own
silent hell in one's own way. Pride is a cold
pudding, but oddly nourishing. The writing, it is
hardly necessary to say, is superb."

G201   Hood, Stuart. "Poor Girls." *Listener* (London), 84 (6
       Aug. 1970), p. 187.

       Stafford's stories can be compared with Andrew Wyeth's
       Christina's World in their "exactitude in the
       description of landscape, of a small-town street or of
       a lodging-house kitchen," in the "concern with the
       longings, miseries and aspirations of ... girls caught
       in poverty and provincialism." Her style is praise-
       worthy for its density: "she contrives to pack her
       sentences with observation, information and sidelong
       comment on life, and is a master of the controlled
       parenthesis." However, she does occasionally lapse
       into magazine writing, and has a "tendency to soft-
       pedal as if to spare her readers' feelings."

G202   Hunsinger, S.K.   "The Test of Solitude." *Christian
       Science Monitor*, 13 March 1969, p. 11.

       While at times Stafford's characters are pitiful,
       "more often they are treated with a sense of irony.
       The author keeps her respectful distance, and so may
       we."

G203   Jackson, Katherine Gauss.   "Books in Brief."
       Harper's, 238 (March 1969), 109.

       Brief, mostly descriptive review.

G204   Janeway, Elizabeth. "The Worlds of Jean Stafford."
       Atlantic, 223 (March 1969), 136-38.

       Stafford's main themes are concerned with "American
       isolation, American awkwardness, American fantasies,
       and the price of American innocence." Janeway com-
       ments at length on four of the stories; she regards
       "Life Is No Abyss" as the best story in the book. A
       particular grace of all the stories is the dialogue:

"There is no one else writing today whose people speak more truly, and more surprisingly."

G205   Kenney, Edwin J., Jr.   "A Fly in Amber."   *Nation*, 208 (14 April 1969), 471-72.

These stories "are the impressive achievement of an established writer." In them, the "mood of the exile and alien, with all his unfulfilled longings to belong somewhere, is fundamental to Miss Stafford's conception of the modern condition."

G206   Lask, T.   "Points East and West."   New York *Times*, 14 Feb. 1969, p. 37.

If we consider anything before Donald Barthelme of value, we will herein find everything we desire in a collection of short stories: "a superior and controlled craftsmanship, human dilemmas uniquely individual, yet common to all of us, backgrounds and situations authentic in themselves and perfect for providing the skeletal structure of her tales, and those insights into human behavior and personality that we call wisdom." Stafford is "especially sensitive to the trapped psyche, the captive mind, parts of us that are victims of circumstance or the will of others or the jerky tricks of fate." Her characters respond by endurance or withdrawal. "But she has ruled out cynicism and pessimism. Rather, her stories argue that we must endure our going hence as our coming hither. They serve as commentary to make that bitter text bearable."

G207   Liberman, Myron M.   *Sewanee Review*, 77 (Summer 1969), 516-21.

These stories fit into two groups: "real stories with sufficient verbal magic to compensate nicely for the absence of explicit casual-temporal logic essential only to the longer fictional forms; and alleged stories which no amount of verbal magic can rescue from a poverty of implied plot and other formal features." However, few of Stafford's stories belong in the latter group, "and even those got out of this pedant a grudging approval."

G208. Malin, Irving. *Commonweal*, 90 (25 April 1969), 174-75.

The last line of "I Love Someone" gives the clue to Stafford's "obsessive themes and images." Her stories "deal with the warped 'management' of life." Her typical protagonist is "an isolated heroine who is afraid to leave her troubled self." These heroines usually refuse to "fight their cages," but when they do, "knowing that they can never really break them open, they see themselves clearly and, moreover, help to liberate us."

G209   Maurer, Robert. "The Deceptive Facade." *Saturday Review*, 52 (1 March 1969), 32.

Although Stafford is a "master of language and the subtlest points of writing," what makes her "one of our finest storytellers is her singular victory of sensibility over technique." These stories rely on "exquisite awareness" rather than the usual artifices of fiction to achieve their effect.

G210   Morse, J. Mitchell. "Brand Names and Others." *Hudson Review*, 22 (Summer 1969), 317-29 [326-27].

"The *New Yorker* publishes excellent stories from time to time, but most of the stories are rather bland and harmless. Jean Stafford's *Collected Stories* are of this kind: very smooth and well-done, but hardly re-readable."

G211   *New York Times Book Review*, 8 June 1969, p. 56.

Brief, mostly descriptive review.

G212   Oates, Joyce Carol. *Book World*, Washington (D.C.) *Post*, 9 Feb. 1969, p. 6.

"Miss Stafford's craftsmanship and her mastery of the short story form are by now so well known that it seems superfluous to praise these stories." Beneath the "delicate and often dazzling ironic surface" of these stories, "there is an undertone of something brutal, something really alarming.... Even in the slightest of these stories, watercolor sketches of shimmering egos attempting to establish themselves as

real, there is a sense of being lost, of being
eternally homesick, of being both unloved and
unloving."

G213   Raban, Jonathan. "Bristle and Twist." *New Statesman*,
        79 (8 May 1970), 667.

"Miss Stafford writes a prose of leisurely, sparkling
distinction; saturated in the atmosphere of place,
superbly responsive to the class and regional voices
of her characters, full of the bristle and twist of
the charged but understated emotional situation." The
title of "I Love Someone" functions "as an epigraph to
the whole collection."

G214   Simon, Marion. "American Exiles." *National Observer*,
        8 (10 March 1969), 23.

These stories are about American exiles and about
"shattered dreams and people imprisoned." However,
they are not sad or filled with despair or self-pity;
on the contrary, because of their wisdom, they are
hopeful: "No matter how you cut it, Miss Stafford
seems to say in each tale, life is no schoolgirl's
dream, but the surest prisoners of all are those
innocents who cling to the idea that it is."

G215   "Some That Survived." *Times Literary Supplement*, 2
        July 1970, p. 701.

Stafford writes about "childhood and the stifling
terrors and guilt which the grown-up world seems to
accept." As to her style, "although the careful and
detached elegance of her sentences may seem to younger
readers far too cloying after a bit, most of us enjoy
a taste of such caviare from time to time."

G216   Stevens, Elisabeth. "Patterns of Involvement and
        Escape." *New Leader*, 52 (3 March 1969), 24-26.

In these stories, "Jean Stafford aptly demonstrates
the possiblilities of the short story--not as a minor
form but as a major summary of experience." However,
in spite of the "grace and control" of Stafford's
style, these stories lack passion, involvement, and
intensity: "After pages of exquisitely prepared pâté,
one hungers for red meat."

G217 *Virginia Quarterly Review*, 45 (Summer 1969), xcii.

Stafford has "extraordinary verbal gifts"; at least
ten of of these thirty stories are masterpieces.

G218 Wagner, Mary Hegel. *America*, 120 (5 April 1969), 426–
27.

"Above all, she is a stylist; her sentences abstracted
from the whole, are beautiful in a way that has almost
become passé." Stafford both accepts and regrets the
world's imperfections, but is concerned merely with
depicting them, without offering any hope for its
improvement.

G219 Wain, John.   "Women's Work."   *New York Review of
Books*, 12 (24 April 1969), 38.

Stafford's stories are linked together by "two strong
threads--the presiding sensibility is always a woman's
and the attitudes are unmistakably American." Her
manner is unhurried: "Confronted with a scene or situation, she moves forward deliberately, possessing it
with her eyes and her mind, taking in all its details,
the meanings it offers, and the meanings it holds
back."

BIO-BIBLIOGRAPHICAL MATERIAL

This section lists bio-bibliographical material on Stafford, and is divided into six subsections: (1) articles, interviews, and reminiscences; (2) references to Stafford in books primarily about others; (3) newspaper stories, editorials, and letters to the editor; (4) articles in reference books; (5) biographical notes in collections; and (6) obituaries. With respect to subdivision 4, only the most recent editions of certain reference works--e.g., *A Library of Literary Criticism* and *Who's Who in America*--are listed because they include all information given in earlier editions. Furthermore, a few reference works are not listed--e.g., *Bibliography of Bibliographies of American Literature* (Charles Nilon) and *The Twentieth Century Novel in English: A Checklist* (E.C.Bufkin)--because these works list only a few items for Stafford, and those few are listed in several other reference works included in this bibliography. The items in all subsections are listed in chronological order, with the exception of the items in subsection 2, which are listed in alphabetical order by the author's last name. If an item herein listed includes a portrait of Stafford, that fact is indicated at the end of the annotation.

1. ARTICLES, INTERVIEWS, REMINISCENCES

H1   "Young U.S. Writers." *Life*, 22 (2 June 1947), 75-76, 78, 81-82.

Groups Stafford with other "literary psychologists"-- Elizabeth Fenwick, Gore Vidal, and Truman Capote, but says that Stafford is the only one "who makes finished art of her material." Portrait.

H2   "Critics Pick the Best Writers." *Quick*, 1 (19 Dec. 1949), 35-36.

Quick's poll of "leading critics" (The *Atlantic Monthly*'s Edward Weeks, the New York *Times*' David Dempsey, the New York *Herald-Tribune*'s John K. Hutchens, the San Francisco *Chronicle*'s Joseph Henry Jackson, and the Chicago *Tribune*'s Frederic Babcock) resulted in Stafford's being named one of the six best writers of the postwar era. Portrait.

H3   Baker, Nina B. "Jean Stafford." *Wilson Library Bulletin*, 25 (15 April 1951), 578.

Gives some general biographical information, along with comments on the reception of Stafford's first two novels. Portrait.

H4   Breit, Harvey. "Talk with Jean Stafford." *New York Times Book Review*, 20 Jan. 1952, p. 18. Rpt. in his *The Writer Observed*. New York: World, 1956, pp. 223-25.

Stafford talks to Breit about her childhood, her first two novels, and about writing in general.

H5   Hutchens,   John K.   "On   an Author."   *New York Herald*
     Tribune Book Review, 24 May 1953, p. 2.

     Reports Stafford's comments on her work. Portrait.

H6   Sheed, Wilfrid.   "Writer as Something Else."   *New York*
     Times Book Review, 4 March 1973, p. 2.

     Stafford and others (Philip Roth, John Updike, Kurt
     Vonnegut, Murray Kempton, and Norman Mailer) talk
     about what they would have been had they not been
     writers.   Stafford describes her adolescent dream to
     become an acrobatic dancer and a Ph.D.

H7   Whitman, Alden.   "Jean Stafford and Her Secretary
     'Harvey' Reigning in Hamptons."   New York *Times*, 26
     Aug. 1973, p. 104.

     Stafford talks about her new novel, *A Parlement of*
     Fowles, which she says is nearing completion, and
     which is the first autobiographical novel she has ever
     written.   "A well-known American poet, with whom I was
     once closely associated, is petrified.   And well he
     should be!   I'm cutting up the poets to a fare-thee-
     well."   Stafford also talks about her writing routine,
     about Henrietta Stackpole (her imaginary secretary),
     and about her plans to go to Boston to teach creative
     writing at Boston University. Four portraits.

H8   Flagg,   Nancy.   "People   to   Stay."   *Shenandoah*,   30
     (Autumn 1979), 65-76.

     Recalls the winter of 1953, which Stafford spent with
     Flagg and her husband at their home in the Virgin
     Islands, while Stafford was waiting out the six weeks
     required to get a divorce.

H9   Moss, Howard.   "Jean: Some Fragments."   *Shenandoah*, 30
     (Autumn 1979),   77-84.   Rpt. in his *Whatever Is*
     Moving. Boston: Little, Brown, 1981, pp. 196-206.

     Reminisces about his friendship with Stafford, which
     began in the early 40's, when he sublet her and
     Lowell's New York apartment, and which lasted until
     her death.   He lists the people he feels she liked
     without qualification: Mrs. Rattray, Saul Steinberg,
     John Stonehill, Peter Taylor, Elizabeth Bowen, and
     Peter De Vries.

H10   Sheed, Wilfrid.   "Miss Jean Stafford."   *Shenandoah*, 20
      (Autumn 1979), 92-99.

      Begins   with   a   description   of   Stafford's   funeral
      service and of the burial of her ashes next to the
      body of A.J. Liebling.   He gives much biographical
      information on her three marriages and on her life
      after Liebling's death.   He emphasizes her growing
      acerbity and attributes it to the frustration of her
      talent.

H11   Straus,   Dorothea.   "Jean   Stafford."   *Shenandoah*, 30
      (Autumn 1979), 85-91.

      Reminisces about her friendship with Stafford, from
      their first meeting in 1950 to their last meeting in
      1979, shortly before Stafford's death.

H12   Taylor, Peter.   "A Commemorative Tribute to Jean
      Stafford.   *Shenandoah*, 30 (Autumn 1979), 56-60.

      Address given on Nov. 13, 1979, at the National
      Academy and Institute of Arts and Letters, New York
      City.

2.   REFERENCES TO STAFFORD IN WORKS PRIMARILY ABOUT OTHERS

H13   Atlas, James.   *Delmore   Schwartz: The   Life   of   an
      American Poet*.   New York: Farrar, Straus and Giroux,
      1977.   Pp. 256, 263-65, 346.

      Schwartz visited Stafford and Lowell in Maine in the
      summer of 1945.   In January, 1946, the Lowells came to
      stay with Schwartz in Cambridge.   Atlas quotes
      Stafford, whom he interviewed for this book, on
      Schwartz's envy of Lowell's background; this event-
      ually led to a fist fight between Lowell and Schwartz,
      into which Stafford had to intervene; after this, the
      Lowells returned to Maine.   Stafford also tells of
      visiting Schwartz years later, not realizing until
      after the visit that Schwartz was "stark, staring
      mad."

H14 Axelrod, Steven Gould. *Robert Lowell: Life and Art*.
     Princeton, N.J.: Princeton University Press, 1978. Pp.
     35-36, 76, 82, 140, 241, 242.

     Lowell met Stafford in the summer of 1937 at a
     writer's conference at the University of Colorado;
     Lowell "converted to his new wife's religion, Roman
     Catholicism"; Stafford worked on *BA* while she and
     Lowell lived with the Tates in Tennessee; their
     marriage was bitterly resolved in 1948. Axelrod also
     mentions some of the works of each that contain
     allusions to each other.

H15 Carr, Virginia Spencer.   *The Lonely   Hunter: A
     Biography of Carson McCullers*. Garden City, N.Y.:
     Doubleday, 1975. Pp. xiii, 234, 547.

     Stafford was with McCullers at Yaddo in the summer of
     1943. Carr includes Stafford in her list of those
     whose "meaningful contribution" enabled her to
     complete this biography.

H16 Cooper, Philip. *The Autobiographical Myth of Robert
     Lowell*.   Chapel Hill: The Univ. of North Carolina
     Press, 1970. Pp. 22, 25-26.

     Cooper gives a few details about Stafford's and
     Lowell's relationship; he mentions the parallels
     between Stafford's "A Country Love Story" and Lowell's
     "The Old Flame."

H17 Fein, Richard J. *Robert Lowell*.   2nd ed. Boston:
     Twayne, 1979. P. 31.

     Fein makes a parenthetical reference to Stafford's
     marriage to and divorce from Lowell in the 1940's.

H18 Haffenden, John.   *The Life of John Berryman*.
     Boston: Routledge & Kegan Paul, 1982. P. 160.

     Mentions the Berrymans' visit to Stafford and Lowell
     in Damariscotta, Maine, in the summer of 1946.

H19 Hamilton, Ian. *Robert Lowell: A Biography*. New York:
     Random, 1982.   Pp. 51-52, 60, 62-69, 72-87, 92-97,
     101-02, 108-12, 114-16, 118-22, 125-33, 138, 145, 155,
     159-60, 182-87, 307-08, 349, 470.

Gives many details about the relationship between Stafford and Lowell, with concentration on their courtship and marriage. Hamilton quotes from many of Stafford's unpublished letters to Robert Lowell, Cecile Starr, Robie Macauley, Allen Tate, and Peter Taylor, written mainly between 1942-1949. He mentions a few of Stafford's and Lowell's allusions to each other in the work of each. Five portraits.

H20 Heymann, C. David. *American Aristocracy: The Lives and Times of James Russell, Amy, and Robert Lowell.* New York: Dodd, Mead, 1980. Pp. 306, 310-11, 313-15, 321, 327, 358-70, 378-80, 415-17, 424, 438, 489, 491, 498.

Heymann acknowledges Stafford as one of the "informed conspirators" who cooperated with him in the writing of this book. He gives many details about the relationship between Stafford and Lowell, from the time they were introduced by Ford Madox Ford in July of 1937, up to Lowell's death in 1973. He paraphrases many of Stafford's unpublished letters to Lowell, and comments extensively on Stafford's and Lowell's allusions to each other in their respective work.

H21 Mills, Hilary. *Mailer: A Biography.* New York: Empire, 1982. P. 137.

Mentions Mailer's association with "a *New Yorker* crowd which centered mainly around A.J. Liebling, Jean Stafford, and Louis Auchincloss."

H22 Olsen, Tillie. *Silences.* New York: Delta/Seymour Lawrence, 1978. Pp. 31-32.

Olsen lists Stafford as one of the many childless women writers of distinguished achievement in 19th and 20th C. British and American literature. If they had had children, Olson asks, "Might there not have been present profound aspects and understandings of human life as yet largely absent in literature?"

H23 Phelps, Robert and Peter Deane. *The Literary Life: A Scrapbook Almanac of the Anglo-American Literary Scene from 1900 to 1950.* New York: Farrar, Straus and Giroux, 1968. Pp. 198, 212.

Portrait of Stafford seated between Robert Lowell and Robert Giroux; include Stafford's *BA* and *ML* in their list of significant books for 1944 and 1947, respectively.

H24   Raffel, Burton. *Robert Lowell.* New York: Frederick Ungar, 1981. Pp. 6, 7, 92, 100.

Mentions the meeting of Stafford and Lowell (1937) and their marriage (1940). Suggests that "The Queen of Heaven" in Lowell's "Home" is a reference to Stafford.

H25   Simpson, Eileen. *Poets in Their Youth: A Memoir.* New York: Random, 1982. Pp. 114-37, 141-46, 150-52, 163-64, 192, 199, 201, 206, 211, 241, 246-47.

Simpson focuses primarily on Stafford as she knew her when Simpson and Berryman visited the Lowells in Maine in July, 1946. (Her sixth chapter is entitled "Damariscotta Mills: Jean and Cal.") Furthermore, she gives a great many details about Stafford's life before and after this time. In addition, Simpson points out autobiographical parallels in several of Stafford's works. Three portraits.

H26   Squires, Radcliffe. *Allen Tate: A Literary Biography.* New York: Pegasus, 1971. P. 157.

Mentions that Stafford accompanied Lowell to join the Tates at Monteagle, Tennessee, sometime during the winter of 1942, and that here Stafford worked on her "best-selling novel," *BA*.

H27   Sokolov, Raymond. *Wayward Reporter: The Life of A.J. Liebling.* New York: Harper and Row, 1980. Pp. 268, 275-81, 283-85, 307-12, 319-20.

Gives a great deal of information on Stafford during her relationship with A.J. Liebling, from the time they first met in the summer of 1956, to the time of Liebling's death on December 21, 1963. During their marriage, Stafford produced little, which she explained by saying it was perhaps because she was happy for the first time in her life. Sokolov acknowledges that without the help of Stafford, who offered him "her home, her records, her memories and herself," the book could not have been written.

3. NEWSPAPER ARTICLES, EDITORIALS, AND LETTERS
   TO THE EDITOR

H28　"O. Henry Prizes Given." New York *Times*, 6 Jan. 1955,
　　　p. 25.

　　　Stafford wins first prize in the 1955 O. Henry Awards
　　　for "In the Zoo," with second prize going to Flannery
　　　O'Connor for "A Circle in the Fire," and third prize
　　　going to Frederick Buechner for "The Tiger."

H29　Hemingway, Mary. Letter to the Editor. *New York*
　　　Review of Books, 10 (25 April 1968), 38.

　　　Sends "Hoorays and thanks to Jean Stafford" for her
　　　review of Parmenia Migel's *Isak Dinesen* (D41).

H30　"15 Are Named to Arts Institute." New York *Times*, 24
　　　Feb. 1970, p. 52.

　　　Stafford is among fifteen artists, writers, and
　　　musicians who have been voted into the National
　　　Institute of Arts and Letters. Of the Institute's 244
　　　members, 120 are in the literature category.

H31　"Biographical Sketches of Persons Chosen for 54th
　　　Annual Pulitzer Prizes." New York *Times*, 5 May 1970,
　　　p. 6.

　　　Biographical sketch. Portrait.

H32　Kihss, Peter. "Report of Sonqmy Incident Wins a
　　　Pulitzer for Hersh." New York *Times*, 5 May 1970, pp.
　　　1, 48.

　　　In this report on the winners of the 1970 Pulitzer
　　　Prize, it is announced that Stafford wins the Pulitzer
　　　for fiction, for her *CS*.

H33　"Pulitzer Awards." New York *Times*, 6 May 1970, p. 42.

　　　In this approving editorial on the Pulitzer awards,
　　　Stafford is one of the six of the seventeen winners
　　　who are mentioned by name.

H34   Calta, Louis.   "Muriel Spark Calls for New Art
      Forms." New York *Times*, 27 May 1970, p. 40.

      At this annual ceremonial meeting of the American
      Academy of Arts and Letters and the National Institute
      of Arts and Letters, Stafford is among the fifteen
      newly elected members formally inducted.

H35   "Whither the Short Story (Or Is It Wither)?" New York
      Times, 21 Nov. 1970, p. 33.

      Stafford is a member of a panel on the future of the
      short story, sponsored by Doubleday & Co., marking the
      publication of the two-volume work, *Fifty Years of the
      American Short Story*. During an informal discussion,
      Stafford told Kay Boyle, "I write for myself and God
      and a few close friends--you and Peter [Taylor] and
      Katherine Anne [Porter] and Eudora [Welty]." Group
      portrait of panelists: Wallace Stegner, Peter Taylor,
      Jean Stafford, Mark Schorer, Kay Boyle, and John
      Barth.

H36   Delatiner, Barbara.   "Mr. Southampton Will Be
      Honored." New York *Times*, 3 June 1973, p. 124.

      Honorary degrees will be awarded to Jean Stafford, Dr.
      H.B. Glass, internationally known geneticist, and W.K.
      Dunwell, Southampton town historian, at Southampton
      College commencement exercises on June 7.

H37   Blaser, Frederick S. Letter to the Editor. New York
      Times, 22 June 1974, p. 28.

      This official of Con-Ed objects to Stafford's June 3
      Op-Ed article on "her harassment of Con Edison"
      (C28). He declares himself "truly outraged at the
      lack of understanding portrayed by a 'supposedly'
      intelligent citizen."

H38   "Mailbag: TV's English Usage." New York *Times*, 29
      Sept. 1974, Sec. II, p. 25.

      In response to Stafford's article on how television is
      "murdering" the English language (C32), Maxwell
      Hamilton makes a comment in verse. Jim Quinn disa-
      grees with Stafford's criticism, saying "The real
      murderer of language is that English teacher, the one

who destroyed for Jean Stafford, and many others, the
pleasure of seeing language as a living entity,
gathering energy and beauty as the people who speak it
grow more various and inventive." Dennis E. Barron
also disagrees with Stafford, saying that "None of
what Miss Stafford criticizes can be regarded as
incorrect by linguists." Andrew Rooney writes to ask
if it is necessary to obtain copyright permission to
use Stafford's phrase "go to hell in a handbasket."

H39   "Members of the Juries for Pulitzer Prizes." New York
       Times, 6 May 1975, p. 34.

       Stafford is a member of the Jury for the Pulitzer
       Prize in Fiction.

H40   "Notes on People." New York *Times*, 16 Sept. 1976, p.
       26.

       Stafford, who has been *Esquire*'s book editor, will be
       replaced by D. Keith Mano; Stafford will continue as a
       contributor.

H41   "Southampton Library Is Planning Comfortable Cubicle
       for Writers." New York *Times*, 19 March 1979, Sect.
       XXI, p. 5.

       Stafford is the honorary chairman of the Writers and
       Artists Committee, which has been planning for the
       last three months for the opening of the John
       Steinbeck Room in the library of Southampton College.

                    4.   ARTICLES IN REFERENCE WORKS

H42   *Current Biography: Who's News and Why, 1951.* Ed. Anna
       Rothe. New York: Wilson, 1951. Pp. 603-04.

       Reprints Baker's article (H3).

H43   Warfel, Harry. *American Novelists of Today.* New
       York: American Book, 1951. P. 401.

Gives brief biography and comments on *BA* and *ML*; says the theme of all Stafford's fiction "is the struggle out of childhood into maturity, and the ceaseless battle of all human beings against isolation."

H44   *Concise Dictionary of American Literature*.   Ed. Robert Fulton Richards.   New York: Philosophical Library, 1955.   P. 212.

Gives a brief biography and overview of Stafford's work up to *CABS* (1953).

H45   *Twentieth Century Authors: A Biographical Dictionary of Literature*.   First supp.   Ed. Stanley J. Kunitz. New York: Wilson, 1955.   Pp. 945-46.

Gives a brief sketch of Stafford's life and career and comments on the critical reception of her three novels and *CABS*.

H46   Gerstenberger,   Donna   and   George   Hendrick.   *The American Novel 1789-1959: A Checklist of Twentieth-Century Criticism*.   Denver: Swallow, 1961.   P. 223.

Lists two critical articles on Stafford.

H47   Herzberg,   Max   J.   *The   Reader's   Encyclopedia   of American   Literature*.   New   York: Crowell, 1962.   P. 1071.

Gives a short overview of Stafford's work through *CABS*.

H48   Benet,   William Rose.   *The Reader's Encyclopedia*.   2nd ed.   New York: Crowell, 1965.   P. 956.

Gives brief overview of Stafford's work through *CABS*.

H49   Hart,   James   David.   *Oxford   Companion   to   American Literature*.   4th ed.   New York: Oxford University Press, 1965.   P. 797.

Gives a brief biography of Stafford and lists her books of fiction.

H50   *Contemporary   Authors: A   Bio-Bibliographical Guide to Current Authors and Their Works*.   Rev. ed.   Ed. James

M. Ethridge and Barbara Kopala. Detroit: Gale, 1967. Vol. I-IV. P. 899.

Gives a brief biography of Stafford, an overview of critical comments on her fiction, and a list of her primary works with a few secondary items.

H51 *A Library of Literary Criticism: Modern American Literature.* 4th ed. Ed. Dorothy Nyren Curley et al. New York: Ungar, 1969. Vol. III. Pp. 194-98.

Gives excerpts from fourteen articles and reviews on six of Stafford's books.

H52 Leary, Lewis. *Articles on American Literature, 1950-1967.* Vol. II. Durham, N.C.: Duke University Press, 1970. P. 491.

Lists six critical articles on Stafford, but one (Greiner's) is incorrect.

H53 Leverenz, Vergene F. In *Encyclopedia of World Literature in the Twentieth Century.* Updated ed. Ed. Wolfgang Bernard Fleischmann. Vol. III. New York: Ungar, 1971. P. 346.

Gives a brief biography of Stafford, followed by an overview of her fiction, with greatest concentration on her short stories. Lists Stafford's books and gives a brief secondary bibliography.

H54 *The Penguin Companion to American Literature.* Ed. Malcolm Bradbury et al. New York: McGraw-Hill, 1971. Pp. 237-38.

Gives a brief biography, and comments on Stafford's three novels, *CABS*, *BC*, and *MH*.

H55 Burke, William Jeremiah and Will D. Howe. *American Authors and Books: 1640 to the Present Day.* 3rd rev. ed. Rev. Irving Weiss and Ann Weiss. New York: Crown, 1972. P. 605.

Lists titles of six of Stafford's books.

H56 Jones, Howard Mumford and Richard M. Ludwig. *Guide to American Literature and Its Backgrounds Since 1890.*

4th ed.   rev.   Cambridge: Harvard University Press,
1972. Pp. 212, 223.

Lists *BA* and *ML* under "The Novel: Latest Phases," and
CABS under "The Short Story in the Twentieth Century."

H57 *Contemporary   Literary   Criticism: Excerpts   from
     Criticism of the Works of Today's Novelists, Poets,
     Playwrights, and Other Creative Writers*. Ed. Carolyn
     Riley. Detroit: Gale, 1975. Vol. IV. Pp. 517-19.

     Gives long excerpts from three articles and reviews on
     Stafford's fiction.

H58 Adelman, Irving and Rita Dworkin. *The Contemporary
     Novel: A Checklist of Critical Literature on the
     British and American Novel Since 1945*.   Metuchen,
     N.J.: Scarecrow, 1972. P. 482.

     Lists five secondary works on Stafford's fiction.

H59 Borklund, Elmer. In *Contemporary Novelists*.   2nd
     ed.   Ed. James Vinson.   New York: St. Martin's,
     1976. Pp. 1279-82.

     Gives a sketch of Stafford's life and career, a list
     of her books, and a critical evaluation of her
     fiction.

H60 *Contemporary Fiction in America and England, 1950-
     1970: A Guide to Information Sources*.   Ed. Alfred F.
     Rosa and Paul A. Eschholz. Detroit: Gale, 1976. P.
     359.

     Lists six of her works of fiction and five secondary
     sources.

H61 *Contemporary   Literary   Criticism: Excerpts   from
     Criticism of Today's Novelists, Poets, Playwrights,
     and Other Creative Writers*.   Ed. Phyllis Carmel
     Mendelson and Dedria Bryfonski.   Detroit: Gale,
     1977. Vol. VII. Pp. 454-60.

     Gives long excerpts from four articles and reviews on
     Stafford's fiction.

H62 *The Reader's Adviser: A Layman's Guide to Literature. Vol. I: The Best in American Fiction, Poetry, Essays, Literary Biography, Bibliography and Reference.* 12th ed. Ed. Sarah L. Prakken. New York: Bowker, 1974. P. 613.

Gives a brief overview of the critical reception of Stafford's work and a brief biography; lists four of her books.

H63 Seymour-Smith, Martin. *Who's Who in Twentieth Century Literature.* New York: Holt, Rinehart and Winston, 1976. P. 35.

Gives a short paragraph on Stafford's books; considers *MH* "perhaps the best of all her books."

H64 Poulton, Jane W. In *Survey of Contemporary Literature.* Rev. ed. Ed. Frank N. Magill. Englewood Cliffs, N.J.: Salem, 1977. Vol. 3. Pp. 1416-18.

Gives plot summaries of several of the stories in *CS*.

H65 Mann, Jeanette. In *Dictionary of Literary Biography. Vol. II: American Novelists Since World War II.* Ed. Jeffrey Helterman and Richard Layman. Detroit: Gale, 1978. Pp. 456-59.

Gives a brief biography of Stafford, but concentrates mainly on each of the novels, with somewhat less on her stories as a whole: "Stafford's major literary contribution has been as an interpreter of human experience within a conventional social system in the period immediately preceding and following World War II, and through the conventions, modes and forms of the realistic tradition. Her reputation rests solely upon the stylistic brilliance and the psychological sureness of her short fiction. Because of general critical neglect of her work, particularly of the novels, her influence can not yet be measured." Lists Stafford's books, one of her periodical articles, and seven secondary works. Portrait of Stafford as an adolescent.

H66 Pownall, David E. *Articles on Twentieth Century Literature: 1954 to 1970.* Vol. VI. New York: Kraus-Thomson, 1978. Pp. 4003-04.

Annotates five critical articles on Stafford.

H67   Trimmer,   Joseph   F.   *The   National   Book   Awards   for
      Fiction: An   Index   to   the   First   Twenty-Five   Years.*
      Boston: Hall, 1978.   Pp. xvi, 25, 35-36, 38, 56, 147,
      150, 180, 235-236.

      Stafford was one of the judges for the 1952 and 1962
      awards.   She was a nominee for *CW* in 1953.   Her *CW*,
      CABS, *BC*, and *CS* were among the books listed as "Best
      Fiction" of 1952, 1953, 1964, and 1969, respectively
      (these books were selected by the editors of the New
      York *Times Book Review*).   *CW* was one of the works of
      "Fiction Appearing on the Best Sellers List for 1952:
      A   composite   list   taken   from   New   York   *Times   Book
      Review*."   She won the Pulitzer Prize for *CS* in 1970.

H68   Leary,   Lewis.   *Articles   on   American   Literature,   1968-
      1975.*   Durham, N.C.: Duke University Press, 1979.   P.
      46.

      Lists four critical articles and reviews in addition
      to those listed in the 1970 edition (see H52).

H69   *Who's   Who   in   America,   1978-79.*   Chicago: Marquis,
      1978.   Vol. II.   P. 3085.

      Lists Stafford's important dates.

H70   Evans,   Patrick.   In   *Great   Writers   of   the   English
      Language.*   Vol. II: *Novelists and Prose Writers.*   Ed.
      James   Vinson   and   D.L.   Kirkpatrick.   New   York:
      Macmillan, 1979.   Pp. 1133-34.   Rpt. in *20th-Century
      American Literature.*   New York: St. Martin's, 1980.
      Pp. 547-48.

      Lists   Stafford's   important   dates   and   her   books;
      comments   on   the   art   of   her   fiction,   finding   *ML* the
      best of the novels.

H71   Corse,   Larry   B.   and   Sandra   Corse.   *Articles   on
      American and British Literature--An Index to Selected
      Periodicals, 1950-1977.*   Chicago: Swallow, 1981.   P.
      139.

      Lists four critical articles for Stafford.

H72   Gunton,   Sharon   R.,   ed.   *Contemporary   Literary
      Criticism: Excerpts   from   Criticism   of   the   Works   of
      Today's   Novelists,   Poets,   Playwrights,   Short   Story*

Writers, Filmmakers, Screenwriters, and Other Creative Writers. Detroit: Gale, 1981. Vol. XIX. P. 430.

Gives excerpt of Voss's criticism on Stafford's short stories (F43).

H73 Mazurkiewicz, Margaret. In *Contemporary Authors: A Bio-Bibliographical Guide to Current Authors and Their Works.* Ed. Ann Evory. New Rev. series. Detroit: Gale, 1981. Vol. III. Pp. 513-14.

Gives a brief sketch of Stafford's life and career, a list of her books, and a sampling of the critical comments that have been made on her work. Lists fourteen biographical/critical sources.

H74 Franklin, Phyllis. In *American Women Writers: A Critical Reference Guide from Colonial Times to the Present.* Ed. Lina Mainiero. New York: Ungar, 1982. Vol. IV. Pp. 149-50.

Gives a brief biography of Stafford, followed by some general comments on her three novels and *CS*; praises Stafford for her "vivid presentation of truth without moral judgment."

H75 Weixlmann, Joe. *American Short-Fiction Criticism and Scholarship, 1959-1977--A Checklist.* Chicago: Swallow, 1982. P. 525.

Lists seven secondary works on Stafford.

5. BIOGRAPHICAL NOTES

H76 Foley, Martha, ed. *The Best American Short Stories, 1945.* Boston: Houghton, 1945. P. 382.

H77 Brickell, Herschel, ed. *Prize Stories of 1947: The O. Henry Awards.* Garden City, New York: Doubleday, 1947. Pp. 294-95.

H78 Foley, Martha, ed. *The Best American Short Stories, 1947.* Boston: Houghton, 1947. P. 510.

H79   Brickell, Herschel, ed. *Prize Stories of 1949: The O.*
      Henry Awards.   Garden City, New York: Doubleday,
      1949. P. 262.

H80   Foley, Martha, ed. *The Best American Short Stories,*
      1949. Boston: Houghton, 1949. P. 320.

H81   Brickell, Herschel, ed. *Prize Stories of 1951: The O.*
      Henry Awards.   Garden City, New York: Doubleday,
      1951. P. 299.

H82   Foley, Martha, ed. *The Best American Short Stories,*
      1951. Boston: Houghton, 1951. P. 356.

H83   _____. *The Best American Short Stories, 1952.*
      Boston: Houghton, 1952. P. 378.

H84   Ludwig, Jack Barry and W. Richard Poirier, eds.
      Stories: British and American.   Boston: Houghton,
      1953. P. 503.

H85   Dimnet, Ernest et al., eds. *The Arts of Living: From*
      the Pages of Vogue.   New York: Simon & Schuster,
      1954. P. 54.

H86   Engle, Paul and Hansford Martin. *Prize Stories, 1954:*
      The O. Henry Awards.   Garden City, New York:
      Doubleday, 1954. P. 216.

H87   Foley, Martha, ed. *The Best American Short Stories,*
      1954. Boston: Houghton, 1954. Pp. 413-14.

H88   Engle, Paul and Hansford Martin, eds. *Prize Stories,*
      1955: The O. Henry Awards. Garden City, New York:
      Doubleday, 1955. P. 15.

H89   Gettman, Royal Alfred and Bruce Harkness, eds. *A Book*
      of Stories.   New York: Holt, Rinehart & Winston,
      1955. Pp. 534-35.

H90   Engle, Paul and Hansford Martin, eds. *Prize Stories,*
      1956: The O. Henry Awards. Garden City, New York:
      Doubleday, 1956. P. 237.

H91   _____. *Prize Stories, 1957: The O. Henry Awards.*
      Garden City, New York: Doubleday, 1957. P. 83.

H92 *First Prize Stories, 1919-1957: From the O. Henry Memorial Awards.* Garden City, New York: Doubleday, 1957. P. 496.

H93 Engle, Paul and Curtis Harnack, eds. *Prize Stories, 1958: The O. Henry Awards.* Garden City, New York: Doubleday, 1958. P. 79.

H94 Foley, Martha and David Burnett, eds. *Best American Short Stories, 1958.* Boston: Houghton, 1958. P. 351.

H95 Engle, Paul, ed. *Prize Stories, 1959: The O. Henry Awards.* Garden City, New York: Doubleday, 1959. P. 105.

H96 Abels, Cyrilly and Margarita G. Smith. *Forty Best Stories from Mademoiselle 1935-1960.* New York: Harper, 1960. P. 312.

H97 Engle, Paul, ed. *Midland: Twenty-Five Years of Fiction and Poetry Selected from the Writing Workshops of the State University of Iowa.* New York: Random, 1961. P. 596.

H98 Gold, Herbert and David L. Stevenson, eds. *Stories of Modern America.* New York: St. Martin's, 1961. P. 351.

H99 Foley, Martha, ed. *The Best American Short Stories, 1965.* Boston: Houghton, 1965. P. 391.

H100 ————. *Fifty Best American Short Stories, 1915-1965.* Boston: Houghton, 1965. P. 397.

H101 Burnett, Hallie, ed. *Sometimes Magic: A Collection of Outstanding Stories for the Teenage Girl.* New York: Platt & Munk, 1966. P. 18.

H102 *First Prize Stories, 1919-1963: From the O. Henry Memorial Awards.* Garden City, New York: Doubleday, 1966. P. 496.

H103 Peden, William, ed. *Twenty-Nine Stories.* 2nd ed. Boston: Houghton, 1967. P. 327.

H104 Steinberg, Erwin R. et al. *Insight: Literature of Imagination.* New York: Noble, 1969. P. 744.

H105   Schulman, L.M., ed. *The Loners: Short Stories About the Young Alienated.* New York: Macmillan, 1970. P. 279.

H106   Auchincloss, Louis, ed. *Fables of Wit and Elegance.* New York: Scribner's, 1972. P. 192.

H107   Schulman, L.M., ed. *Travelers: Stories of Americans Abroad.* New York: Macmillan, 1972. P. 285.

H108   Oates, Joyce Carol, ed. *Scenes from American Life: Contemporary Short Fiction.* New York: Random, 1973. P. 151.

H109   Foley, Martha, ed. *200 Years of Great American Short Stories.* Boston: Houghton, 1975. P. 732.

H110   Smart, William, ed. *Women & Men, Men & Women: An Anthology of Short Stories.* New York: St. Martin's, 1975. P. 363.

H111   Manley, Seon and Gogo Lewis. *Sisters of Sorcery: Two Centuries of Witchcraft Stories by the Gentle Sex.* New York: Lothrop, 1976. Pp. 218-19.

H112   Hamalian, Linda and Leo Hamalian, eds. *Solo: Women on Woman Alone.* New York: Delacorte, 1977. Pp. 362-63.

H113   Solomon, Barbara H., ed. *The Experience of the American Woman: 30 Stories.* New York: New American, 978. P. 447.

H114   Abrahams, William, ed. *Prize Stories 1980: The O. Henry Awards.* Garden City, New York: Doubleday, 1980. P. 422.

6. OBITUARIES

H115   Chicago *Tribune*, 28 March 1979, Sec. 3, p. 5.

H116   Lask, Thomas. New York *Times*, 28 March 1979, Sec. B, p. 12, portrait; rpt. New York *Times Biographical Service*, 10 (March 1979), 381-82.

H117 Smith, J.Y. Washington (D.C.) *Post*, 29 March 1979, Sec. B, p. 6. Portrait.

H118 *Newsweek*, 93 (9 April 1979), 86. Portrait.

H119 *Publisher's Weekly*, 215 (9 April 1979), 26.

H120 *Time*, 113 (9 April 1979), 78.

H121 *AP Bookman's Weekly*, 63 (16 April 1979), 2942.

H122 *Current Biography: Who's News and Why, 1979*. Ed. Charles Moritz. P. 473.

H123 *Contemporary Authors: A Bio-Bibliographical Guide to Current Writers in Fiction, General Nonfiction, Poetry, Journalism, Drama, Motion Pictures, Television, and Other Fields*. Ed. Frances Carol Locher. Detroit: Gale, 1980. Pp. 85-88, 560.

H124 *Something About the Author: Facts and Pictures About About Authors and Illustrators of Books for Young People*. Ed. Anne Commire. Vol. XXII. Detroit: Gale, 1981. P. 218.

INDEX

This index is keyed to all sections of this bibliography and lists: (1) the titles of all works by Jean Stafford, in capital letters; (2) the names of all authors, editors, and translators of books that contain material by and about Jean Stafford; and the names of all authors of articles and reviews that pertain to her work; (3) the titles of all books and periodicals that contain material by and about Jean Stafford; (4) the subjects mentioned in the annotations, including all titles and personal names. Subject names are so identified--e.g., "Greene, Graham (subject)"; subject titles are listed with the author's last name in parentheses following--e.g., *The Comedians* (Greene)." With respect to category 1, item numbers for reviews of Stafford's books are given at the end of each book-title entry.

Abels, Cyrilly, B38, H96
Abrahams, William, B20, B31, B48, F52, H114
Acton, Harold (subject), D102
Ada (Nabokov), D54
Adams, Abigail and John (subject), D94
Adelman, Irving, H58
The Adolescent in the American Novel: 1920-1980, F45
After Julius (Howard), D26
After the Lost Generation: A Critical Study of the Writers of Two Wars, F1
Against Our Will (Brownmiller), D91
L'Âge du roman américain, F78
The Age of the American Novel: The Film Aesthetic of Fiction Between the Two Wars, F26
Aldous Huxley (Huxley), D28
Aldridge, John W., F1-2
Allen Tate: A Literary Biography, H26
Alliluyeva, Svetlana (subject), D60
Alther, Lisa (subject), D96
America, G17, G145, G173, G218
American Aristocracy: The Lives and Times of James Russell, Amy, and Robert Lowell, F20
American Short-Fiction Criticism and Scholarship, 1959-1977-- A Checklist, H75
American Authors and Books: 1640 to the Present Day, H55
The American Coast, C15
American Literature in the Twentieth Century, F38
The American Novel 1789-1959: A Checklist of Twentieth-Century Criticism, H46
American Novelists of Today, H43
American Novelists Since World War II, H65
American Prefaces, B1
American Quarterly, F16
American Scholar, E3
American Short Stories Since 1945, B10, F65
American Short Story, F31
The American Short Story: A Critical Survey, F43
The American Short Story: Front Line in the National Defense of Literature, F29